D1001795

ROBERT F. KENNEDY

MAKERS OF AMERICA

ROBERT F. KENNEDY

Promise for the Future

ARLENE SCHULMAN

Facts On File, Inc.

Robert F. Kennedy: Promise for the Future

Copyright © 1998 by Arlene Schulman

All rights reserved. No part of this book may be reproduced or utilized in any form or by any means, electronic or mechanical, including photocopying, recording, or by any information storage or retrieval systems, without permission in writing from the publisher. For information contact:

Facts On File, Inc.
11 Penn Plaza
New York NY 10001

Library of Congress Cataloging-in-Publication Data

Schulman, Arlene.
    Robert F. Kennedy : promise for the future / Arlene Schulman.
        p.   cm. — (Makers of America)
    Includes bibliographical references (p.   ) and index.
    ISBN 0-8160-3674-8 (acid-free paper)
    1. Kennedy, Robert F., 1915–1968.   2. Legislators—United States—
Biography.   3. United States.   Congress.   Senate—Biography.
    I. Title.   II. Series: Makers of America (Facts on File, Inc.)
E840.8K4S38   1998
973.922′092—dc21   97-20610
[B]

Facts On File books are available at special discounts when purchased in bulk quantities for businesses, associations, institutions or sales promotions. Please call our Special Sales Department in New York at (212) 967-8800 or (800) 322-8755.

You can find Facts On File on the World Wide Web at
http://www.factsonfile.com

Text design by Cathy Rincon
Cover design by Matt Galemmo

Printed in the United States of America

MP FOF 10 9 8 7 6 5 4 3 2 1

This book is printed on acid-free paper.

Trails of troubles,
Roads of battles,
Paths of victory,
We shall walk.
—Bob Dylan

CONTENTS

ACKNOWLEDGMENTS

With a deep bow of gratitude for their assistance, the author wishes to thank the respective staffs of The James Thurber House, the Inwood branch of the New York Public Library, the John F. Kennedy Library, and Bedford-Stuyvesant Restoration.

INTRODUCTION

When he first came to the Senate, as the junior senator from New York, Robert F. Kennedy knew little about Cesar Chavez, the head of the United Farm Workers Organizing Committee, and the conditions of migrant grape workers in California. Chavez had urged workers to protest poor working conditions and win recognition of their union by grape growers. But when the workers did protest, farm owners fired them and had the laborers arrested. They were attacked by dogs and sprayed with pesticides. As a member of the migratory labor subcommittee of the Senate Labor Committee, Kennedy flew to Delano, California, in 1966 to meet with Chavez and his workers and to listen to their testimony. He supported Chavez and spoke about the farmworkers' union's cause in Congress.

Chavez began a 25-day fast to protest violence during the farmworkers' strike in March of 1968. Kennedy was the only political figure invited to join Chavez when he ended his fast, just before Kennedy was to announce his candidacy for the presidency. Some thought that if Kennedy went, he would lose votes in California. Kennedy went anyway, and he greeted Chavez and 6,000 of his followers. Chavez broke his fast by sharing communion bread with Kennedy at a mass that day. Kennedy called Chavez "a hero for our times." Said Cesar Chavez: "There was a kind of mystical aura about him, something that was electrifying and almost religious in its intensity."

1

COMING TO AMERICA: THE KENNEDYS AND FITZGERALDS OF BOSTON

Immigrants coming to the United States, whether hundreds of years ago or today, have one thing in common—hope. Pilgrims sailing from England, looking for religious freedom; Jews fleeing from Nazi Germany during World War II; Cubans escaping the dictatorship of Fidel Castro; Italians, Mexicans, Africans, or Russians searching for work—all have dreamed of a land where they could be free of poverty and oppression. They longed for well-paying jobs, decent homes, better education, and a chance at success. The Irish were no different.

Prior to 1921, Ireland was governed by Great Britain, a predominantly Protestant nation. The Irish were predominantly Catholic, and under British law Catholic land ownership and education were severely restricted; Catholics were not allowed to vote or hold political office. The economy of Ireland depended on the potato. Almost every boy in rural Ireland was raised to be a potato farmer. But in 1845, Ireland's potatoes became infected with a deadly fungus. The Great Famine, as it came to be known, killed off half of Ireland's potato crop. Over 750,000 Irish died of starvation and disease in one-room cottages lacking heat and hot water. Also dying were the cows, sheep, and goats that the Irish depended on for meat, milk, and cheese.

With little hope left for survival in their own land, many Irish decided to emigrate. They thought of America as the land of opportunity, particularly Boston, Massachusetts, where a large community of their countrymen had settled. People sold what few possessions they had so they could afford the price of passage—the equivalent of $12. Sometimes their landlords paid for their tickets in order to get rid of them. More than a million Irish emigrated between 1846 and 1855. Ships were filthy and crowded, and diseases like typhus swept through the passengers' quarters. Many died on the voyage over, but the hope of a better life in a new country kept many more alive.

Patrick Kennedy, Jr., watched the ships sail for America from the docks of New Ross, a small seaport village on the coast of Ireland. He was from nearby Dunganstown, one of four children of a farmer and his wife. The Kennedys were affected only indirectly by the Great Famine. They farmed 80 acres of land that was so productive that the landlord kept raising their rent to make up for the money he was losing on poorer farms. But Patrick Kennedy did not want to work the land for the rest of his life. So, in 1849, when he was 25, he decided to move to Boston.

Kennedy purchased a ticket and boarded a ship that took 40 days to reach his destination. He would never see his family again. While on board, he met 27-year-old Bridget Murphy, who was traveling with her family. They became engaged, and he told her that as soon as he saved up enough money he would marry her.

Patrick Kennedy arrived in Boston to find another kind of poverty. One out of every six Irish in Boston was dying of starvation, and in a single hundred-day period, a thousand children under the age of five died of cholera. The Irish were living in run-down tenements overflowing with people. In one building, 24 adults, 13 children, and the customers of a bar on the first floor shared a single bathroom. While there were jobs in Boston, the Irish were used mainly as cheap labor. The women worked as maids and were called "biddies" and "kitchen canaries," while the men, mockingly labeled "micks" and "paddies," worked in construction, labored on the docks, or shoveled coal. Boston's well-to-do were descendants of the Protestant English, and they controlled politics, law, and finance in the city. Irish immigrants seeking better jobs or housing were confronted by signs that read "NO IRISH NEED APPLY" or "NONE NEED APPLY BUT AMERICANS."

"This country offered great advantages, even then," Robert Kennedy said more than a century later. "But one familiar with the story of the Irish here would underrate the difficulties they faced after landing in the United States. As the first of the racial minorities, our forefathers were subject to every discrimination found wherever discrimination is known."[1]

Patrick Kennedy's first job was making barrels and parts for covered wagons, working 12 hours a day, seven days a week. In 1849, nine months after he left Ireland, he had saved up enough money to marry Bridget Murphy. He was 26 and she was 28. The newlyweds resided in East Boston, where Bridget gave birth to three daughters, Mary, Margaret, and Johanna. Their last child—the only boy—was born in 1858. They named him Patrick Joseph. Less than a year later, Patrick Kennedy contracted cholera. Ten years after arriving in America, Patrick Kennedy died, as poor as when he landed.

Bridget Kennedy was left alone to raise and support the children. She found a job in a small shop and managed to save enough money to open her own store, where she sold groceries and household items. All of her children worked there, selling, packing, and making deliveries. Patrick Joseph dropped out of school as a teenager in order to earn money working on the Boston docks. When he was 22, he bought a run-down saloon, and by the time he was 25, he had saved up enough money to open a business that sold beer to other establishments. His bar quickly became one of the most popular in East Boston. Ironically, he himself drank little.

Bars provided the Irish with a place to meet and relax after a day's hard labor. As centers of the Irish community, the corner pub and political base were often the same place. They doubled as campaign headquarters for local political candidates, with back rooms serving as dealmaking centers where mayors and congressmen were chosen. Patrick Joseph, called P. J., offered advice, mediated disputes, arranged job interviews, lent money, and sold beer and wine for both weddings and wakes. His bar soon became the center of politics in East Boston, and within a few years he was able to buy two more. Before he turned 30, he started an importing firm called P. J. Kennedy and Company, bringing in liquors from Europe and

South America. He later owned part of a local coal company and Boston's only Irish-controlled bank, Columbia Trust.

When the popular Kennedy turned 27 in 1885, he decided to run for political office. He was elected to the Massachusetts legislature and served five one-year terms from 1886 to 1890. In 1891, he was elected to the state senate, serving three one-year terms. He soon married Mary Augusta Hickey, whom he called Mame. Mary's father was also a wealthy bar owner, and her brother was the mayor of Brockton. In 1888, Mary Hickey Kennedy gave birth to a son named Joseph Patrick. Two months later, the child's grandmother, Bridget Kennedy, died at the age of 67.

P. J. Kennedy had found his calling in politics. He had a motto engraved on a plaque above his desk that read "I shall pass through this world but once. Any kindness I can do, or goodness show, let me do it now—for I shall not pass this way again." He served as Boston's election commissioner for five years and was a delegate to the Democratic National Conventions in 1892, 1896, and 1900. By 1900, the Irish ruled Boston politics, and P. J. Kennedy was one of the best dealmakers around. His motto was "Win at all costs."

P. J. Kennedy served with John Francis Fitzgerald of the North End of Boston as one of four members of the Board of Strategy, and both men were state senators in 1893. Though they were rivals for political power, their families met often during the summer at Old Orchard Beach, Maine, when the Democratic party of Boston held its annual outing. John Francis Fitzgerald, born in 1863, was one of eight children—seven boys and a girl—whose father owned a grocery store and liquor business. He attended Harvard Medical School but had to drop out after a year to support his family when his father died. Fitzgerald, known as "Honey Fitz," became a canny politician who often made front-page news. Active in neighborhood politics, he set up an office where a clerk filed applications from constituents seeking employment. A state senator for two terms in 1893 and 1894, he ran successfully for the U.S. Congress three times, becoming the only Democratic congressman from New England and the only Catholic in the House of Representatives. Fitzgerald was the first Boston mayor whose parents had been born in Ireland. He was elected to that post twice, serving for six years. The song "Sweet Adeline" became his trademark, and he sang it over and over for years at public events. During campaigns, his face was plastered on billboards all over town. "Honey Fitz" was as popular as P. J. Kennedy. A tireless campaigner, he distributed turkeys at Christmas and attended dances, beauty pageants, weddings, and funerals. He scanned the obituaries and wrote a personal letter to each widow. Fitzgerald's slogan was "Work harder than anyone else" and "A bigger, better, busier Boston." He had a fantastic memory for quotations and anecdotes and loved to recite Boston's history and current events. According to a poem about him that appeared in a local newspaper:

> Honey Fitz can talk you blind
> On any subject you can find.
> Fish and fishing, motorboats,
> Railroads, streetcars, getting votes,
> Proper ways to open clams,
> How to cure existing shams;
> State Street, Goo-Goos, aeroplanes,
> Malefactors, thieving gains,
> Local transportation rates,
> How to run the nearby states;
> On all these things, and many more.[2]

Presidents William McKinley, William Howard Taft, and Franklin Delano Roosevelt invited Fitzgerald to the White House many times. Fitzgerald died in 1950 when he was 87. In 1947 his grandson John Fitzgerald Kennedy took over his old seat in Congress. Fitzgerald predicted that John would one day become president.

P. J. and Mary Kennedy lived a comfortable life, served by maids and cooks, sailing on their yacht, and vacationing in Palm Beach, Florida. But as prominent and wealthy as they were, they were not permitted into the political and social clubs run by Protestants. They were determined that their son, Joseph, obtain the best education possible. Instead of attending the local Catholic school, young Joe Kennedy was enrolled in Boston Latin, an exclusive Protestant school attended by many of the sons of prominent Boston families. A friendly boy with blue eyes, freckles, and red hair, he was popular with his schoolmates. He started working when he was 12, delivering hats via a horse-drawn carriage with a driver, and he also sold

At Old Orchard Beach, Maine, in 1906 (left to right): Second from left: P. J. Kennedy, Rose Fitzgerald, and Honey Fitz. Joseph P. Kennedy, Sr., the father of John and Robert Kennedy, is second from the right. (John F. Kennedy Library)

newspapers. His grades were poor to average, but he was an outstanding baseball player, holding the highest batting average on the school team in his senior year. He was also elected class president. He went on to Harvard University, where, he later admitted, he was not a great student. "I did so poorly in a course in banking and finance," he told *Fortune* magazine after estimating his wealth at $250 million, "that I had to drop out of it after one semester."[3]

Joe Kennedy first met Rose Fitzgerald in 1895, when he was seven and she was five. Rose remembered him as a serious young man but also recalled that as a teenager "he smiled and laughed easily and had a big, spontaneous, and infectious grin that made everybody in sight want to smile, too."[4] Rose graduated from Dorchester High School at the age of 15 with the best grades in her class. She was also voted the most beautiful girl in the school by her senior class. Joe and Rose soon began to take a special interest in one another, but Rose's father, the mayor of Boston, forbade her to see Joe. Mayor Fitzgerald thought that Joe Kennedy was beneath Rose and tried to interest his daughter in other young men. But the young people managed to meet at dances and at parties and go for long walks. Rose wanted to go to college, and her preference was Wellesley, a small private women's college 20 miles west of Boston. But her father insisted that she attend convent school, like most young Catholic women of her time. In 1908, he sent her to Holland, where she spent a year in a convent, studying French and German and learning how to run a household. While she was away, Rose kept up a secret correspondence with Joe Kennedy. When she arrived back in the United States, she attended the Sacred Heart Academy in New York City for a year. She returned home to Boston as the city's newest debutante, and her coming-out party was attended by the governor, two congressmen, and over 400 other guests. She quickly jumped into the role of hostess at political events, since her mother was not interested in politics. She played the piano when her father sang "Sweet Adeline," and she founded the Ace of Clubs, a private club for Irish-Catholic women that became very popular.

Joe Kennedy graduated from Harvard in the class of 1912, and then, through his father's connections, he was hired as a state bank examiner in Massachusetts, earning $1,500 a year. He traveled extensively, investigating banks and bank operations and examining their records. Soon he knew the financial structure of the banking business better than the bankers did themselves.

His father's bank, Columbia Trust, was on the verge of being taken over by First Ward National Bank. P. J. Kennedy consulted Joe on how to handle the situation. Joe Kennedy found a group of backers and raised enough money to save the bank. At 25, he became the youngest bank president in the country. A local newspaper reporter asked him what he wanted out of life. "I want to be a millionaire by the age of thirty-five," he replied.[5]

But first, Joe Kennedy wanted to marry Rose Fitzgerald. Mayor Fitzgerald still did not think much of his rival's son, but once Joe graduated from Harvard and became a bank president, the mayor began to reconsider. Finally, he gave his blessing, and the couple was married on October 7, 1914.

Rose and Joe Kennedy moved into a seven-room house at 83 Beals Street in Brookline, Massachusetts. Brash, ambitious, and eager for an opportunity to make money, Kennedy began working as a stock market manager at the Boston branch of the brokerage house of Hayden, Stone and Company. He learned quickly how to work the market to buy and sell stocks, and his earnings were estimated at $2 million in the early 1920s. "Joe Kennedy saw early what made the power and gentility he wanted," commented a critic. "It wasn't talent, it was ancient riches. Power came from money."[6] He soon purchased 31 movie theaters throughout New England. "My husband changed jobs so fast, I simply never knew what business he was in," recalled Rose Kennedy.[7] In 1919, Prohibition went into effect, outlawing the importing, sale, and manufacture of alcohol in the United States. It is not entirely clear what role Kennedy played during Prohibition, but there is speculation that he bought and sold liquor illegally. Kennedy family members have denied this, but organized crime figures later testified that Joe Kennedy was a major bootlegger. Sam Giancana told a friend that Kennedy "was one of the biggest crooks who ever lived."[8] Frank Costello insisted that he "helped Joe Kennedy get rich." Kennedy obtained licenses to import liquor for medicinal purposes and stockpiled it in warehouses. When it became legal to sell liquor again in 1933, Kennedy was one of

The Kennedys at Hyannis in 1931 (left to right): Robert; John; Eunice; Jean; Pat; Kathleen; Joe, Jr.; and Rosemary Kennedy, with Joe and Rose Kennedy in the middle (John F. Kennedy Library)

the first distributors, and he earned millions. He set up trust funds for his children, with each automatically receiving $1 million or more on their 21st birthday.

While Joe handled the business deals, Rose raised nine children. "I looked on child rearing not only as a work of love and duty, but as a profession that was fully as interesting and challenging as any honorable profession in the world, and one that demanded the best I could bring to it," she wrote in her autobiography. "What greater aspiration and challenge are there for a mother than the hope of raising a great son or daughter?"[9] In 1915, the couple's first child, Joseph Patrick Kennedy, Jr., was born. "Is he going into politics?"Honey Fitz was asked. "Well . . . of course he is going to be President of the United States, his mother and father have already decided that he is going to Harvard, where he will play on the football and baseball teams and incidentally take all the scholastic honors," the mayor answered. "Then he's going to be a captain of industry until it's time for him to be President for two or three terms."[10]

Joe, Jr., was followed in 1917 by John Fitzgerald Kennedy, named after Rose's father. Rosemary was born a year later, followed by Kathleen in 1920, Eunice Mary in 1921, Patricia in 1924, Robert Francis in 1925, Jean Ann in 1928, and Edward Moore (called Ted) in 1932. All in all, these children were to have a greater impact on 20th-century U.S. politics than any other family in the nation.

Notes

1. Speech, Friendly Sons of St. Patrick of Lackawanna County, March 17, 1964.
2. Rose Fitzgerald Kennedy, *Times to Remember* (Garden City, N.Y.: Doubleday, 1974), p. 10.
3. Peter Collier and David Horowitz, *The Kennedys: An American Drama* (New York: Summit Books, Simon & Schuster, 1984), p. 36.
4. Kennedy, *Times to Remember*, p. 57.
5. Collier and Horowitz, *The Kennedys*, p. 37.
6. Doris Kearns Goodwin, *The Fitzgeralds and the Kennedys: An American Saga* (New York: Simon & Schuster, 1987), p. 232.
7. Goodwin, *The Fitzgeralds and the Kennedys*, p. 303.

8. John H. Davis, *The Kennedys: Dynasty and Disaster* (New York: McGraw-Hill, 1984), p. 57.
9. Kennedy, *Times to Remember*, p. 76.
10. Goodwin, *The Fitzgeralds and the Kennedys*, p. 262.

2

THE YOUNG KENNEDYS

Joe Kennedy's movie studio, Film Booking Office of America, produced such little-remembered films as *Hot Hooves* and *The Dude Cowboy*. Kennedy raised money to buy another chain of theaters and was responsible for merging the studios that became R.K.O. By the summer of 1929, Kennedy had produced 76 films and earned over $6 million. He was still only 41 years old. Along with his film business, he purchased large office buildings in New York City and then bought the Chicago Merchandise Mart for close to $13 million. Each year he took in rents that far exceeded what he had paid for the building. Before the Great Depression of 1929, when many lost millions, Kennedy made huge profits, estimated at as much as $15 million, by selling off his stocks. By 1950, his wealth was estimated at $400 million.

Heavily involved in the movie industry, Kennedy opened an office in Hollywood in the late 1920s. He lived most of the time in Beverly Hills, California, gaining a reputation for affairs with glamorous women, notably the film actress Gloria Swanson—an affair that she detailed in her autobiography. Rose, whatever she knew, never discussed her husband's philanderings. Joe Kennedy called home nearly every day, and on Sundays he spoke to his children as they lined up in age order to talk with him. He regularly wrote them letters filled with advice and praise. The Kennedys owned three homes. They spent summers in Hyannis Port in Cape Cod, Massachusetts, in a house containing 11 bedrooms, nine bathrooms, and a movie theater in the basement. They had another home in Bronxville, New York, and a third in Palm Beach, Florida. They had moved to the 20-room Bronxville house in 1926 because Kennedy, tired of being looked on as inferior by Boston's upper class, had decided to live elsewhere—and at the same time he wanted to be closer to his Wall Street office. Before the Kennedys left Boston, a friend asked Joe, "What is it you really want?" He replied, "Everything."[1]

Assisted by governesses, nurses, housekeepers, and cooks, Rose Kennedy ran an organized household. She arranged a system of file cards with index tabs to keep track of her children's vaccinations, eye exams, and dental appointments. The Kennedy children were weighed every Saturday night, and they brushed after every meal. "I remember it as part of the morning drill. She'd always come down, in her robe, for breakfast with us, to make sure we had the right food and ate it and then brushed our teeth," recalled Eunice Kennedy Shriver, the fifth of the Kennedy children. "There was a downstairs bathroom and we'd file in and out one by one. Then stand inspection for spots on our clothes and general neatness."[2] Rose was a religious woman who attended church regularly, including mass on Sundays and on holy days. Each child took a turn at saying grace before meals. Calisthenics were performed at seven in the morning, and the children took golf, tennis, swimming, and dance lessons. "We were really organized," recalls Eunice. "We went to dancing lessons once a week, which bored us, but we did turn out to be good dancers. She wanted us to swim and play tennis and golf properly, so schedules of lessons were laid out, which sometimes were a drag, but we did develop the skills and they've been assets."[3] Rose pinned notes to her dress listing the day's events. She collected items of interest in scrapbooks and notebooks, and she hung up a bulletin board where she pinned newspaper and magazine clippings for the children to see. She selected books that she expected them to read, a list that included *Peter Pan, Black Beauty, Uncle Tom's Cabin, Arabian Nights, King Arthur and the Round Table*, and *Treasure Island*.

Rose placed clocks in every room and expected the children to be on time for meals. When they were asked a question at the dinner table, they were expected to have an intelligent answer. Dinners were formal affairs when their father was in town, and the conversation often centered on world politics. Joe Kennedy held many strong opinions, and he encouraged his children to argue with him. "He was generous to a fault, but woe unto him who made the mistake of taking advantage of it," said Ted Kennedy, the youngest of the nine. "Dad was a taskmaster, too. He was also quick to admonish us for errors. He tolerated a mistake once, but never a second time. Because he was interested, because he did care, because he wanted to help, he brought out the best in each of us. We were ashamed to do less than our best because of our respect and feelings for him."[4]

John Kennedy said, "My father wasn't around as much as some fathers when I was young; but, whether he was there or not, he made his children feel that they were the most important things in the world to him. He was so terribly interested in everything we were doing. He held up standards for us, and he was very tough when we failed to meet those standards."[5]

Summers in Hyannis were filled with visitors, games of touch football, swimming, and sailing races. Later, both John and Robert bought houses next to their father's. "The most important thing was to win—don't come in second or third—that doesn't count—but win, win, win," said Eunice Kennedy Shriver of her father. He told his children over and over again, "Kennedys don't cry."[6]

"He was this extraordinary figure that was trying to keep the blowtorch on you, in terms of your own kind of abilities, and was quite willing to point out your deficiencies and challenge you to do better," said Ted Kennedy.[7]

Joe, Jr., was very much like his father—brash, ambitious, the leader of his brothers and sisters, and the one his father had the greatest hopes for. It was Joe who named the family the "Kennedy clan." Joe, Jr., and John, who was called Jack, were two years apart and were friendly rivals, calling each other "Brother." Rose dressed them alike. But John was physically the weakest. At birth he had not been expected to live and had been given the last rites. His childhood ailments ranged from scarlet fever to Addison's disease (an illness affecting the adrenal glands) to back problems. The third child, Rosemary, was eventually diagnosed as suffering from mental retardation. So Kathleen became the "oldest" sister. Nicknamed "Kick" for her vivacious personality, she was five years younger than

Young Robert Kennedy (John F. Kennedy Library)

Joe and three years younger than John. She was outspoken, full of fun, a good athlete, and a graceful dancer with a great sense of style and taste in clothes. "She was the apple of my eye," her father wrote. She and Joe were the closest of the brothers and sisters. "They were the pick of the litter," says one Kennedy friend, "the ones the old man thought would write the story of the next generation."[8] The rest of the children formed close relationships with each other, more so than with outsiders. "We liked each other more than we liked other people, but I suppose that's natural," Eunice Kennedy Shriver said.[9]

The third son, Robert Francis Kennedy, was born on November 25, 1925, following the birth of four daughters. His maternal grandmother said, "He's stuck by himself in a bunch of girls. He'll be a sissy."[10] He was eight years younger than his brother John. While his brothers and sisters were outgoing and athletic, Robert was quiet, shy, and a little awkward. Rose called him "her little pet." Joe Kennedy focused his attention on the trio of Joe, Jr., John, and Kathleen while Rose looked after the others. "I was the seventh of nine children," Robert

Kennedy once said, "and when you come from that far down you have to struggle to survive." "Bobby had a lot going against him," said Lem Billings, a longtime friend of the Kennedys. "He was small, rather shy and uncertain and lost, as he was in the middle of a flock of sisters; lacking in identity, he had a hard time asserting himself."[11]

Bobby sold magazines, including the *Saturday Evening Post* and the *Ladies' Home Journal*, from door to door as other children did—except that he had the chauffeur drive him in the family Rolls-Royce until Rose put a stop to it. "Jack has certainly had the most outstanding success. . . . Bobby is a different mold. He does not seem to be interested particularly in reading or sailing or stamps. He does a little work in all three, but no special enthusiasm," Rose Kennedy wrote in a letter to her husband.[12] Bobby attended 10 different elementary and secondary schools. "What I remember most about growing up," he later recalled, "was going to a lot of different schools, always having to make new friends, and that I was very awkward. I dropped things and fell down all the time. I had to go to the hospital a few times for stitches in my head and my leg. And I was pretty quiet most of the time. I didn't mind being alone."[13]

He was the most devout of Joe and Rose's children, saying prayers in the morning and evening and attending mass three times a week. Lem Billings recalled, "As a child, Bobby was the smallest and the least articulate of all the boys. Nothing came easy to him, but he never stopped trying. He willed himself into the water to learn to swim, and he willed himself onto the football field. And where John rebelled against his parents' obsession with punctuality, Bobby was always on time for everything—for meals, church, and school. Yet the funny thing was that while he secured his mother's love by being so good, so gentle and so religious, it made him even more invisible to his father." "While they all knew what was expected of them," his mother recalled, "Bobby really worked at it."[14]

During the early 1930s, Joe Kennedy was becoming more and more involved in politics. Franklin D. Roosevelt, the popular governor of New York, was running for president in 1932, and Kennedy decided to help him get elected. "I was really worried," Kennedy later said. "I knew that big, drastic changes had to be made in our economic system and I felt that

Roosevelt was the one who could make those changes. I wanted him in the White House for my own security and the security of our kids—and I was ready to do anything to help elect him."[15] Kennedy contributed $25,000 to the Roosevelt campaign, lent Roosevelt $50,000, and raised $100,000 from his friends. In exchange for his support, Roosevelt appointed Kennedy chairman of the newly formed Securities and Exchange Commission. In this post, Kennedy helped establish regulations to protect stock purchasers from fraud and corruption. He resigned in 1935 after winning praise from both business groups and political reformers. With Roosevelt's reelection campaign looming, Kennedy wrote a book called *I'm for Roosevelt*, noting in the introduction that "I have no political ambitions for myself or for my children and I put down these few thoughts about our President, conscious only of my concern as a father, for the future of his family and my anxiety as a citizen that the facts about the President's philosophy be not lost in a fog of unworthy emotion."[16] Kennedy then campaigned to become ambassador to Britain. It was the most prestigious post for an ambassador and one that was most unusual for an Irish Catholic to hold. It would give Kennedy the status he craved. Roosevelt offered the job to an overjoyed Kennedy at the end of 1937. He had "arrived" in American society at last.

In 1938, Kennedy moved to London. He planned to be involved in American foreign policy, but his views were different from those of President Roosevelt. Kennedy was considered an isolationist who believed that the United States should not get involved in the affairs of other nations. He misread the political situation in Europe, predicting that there would not be a war and doubting that German dictator Adolf Hitler was dangerous. Even after Hitler occupied Austria and Czechoslovakia, Kennedy was among those who believed that Hitler should be pacified, not opposed, and his view was considered to be an endorsement of Hitler. In 1939, Germany invaded Poland, setting off World War II. Kennedy advised Roosevelt to stay out of the conflict, even after France surrendered in May of 1940, leaving Britain to fight alone. Kennedy then announced that democracy was finished in England and returned home. In June 1941, Germany invaded the Soviet Union; six months later, the Japanese attacked Pearl Harbor, bringing the United States into the war.

Kennedy was not well liked in England, being perceived as an opportunist. While British royalty were well-mannered and reserved, he was blunt and arrogant, and he once referred to the queen as "a cute trick." During Kennedy's tenure U.S. secretary of the interior Harold Ickes wrote in his diary, "We have sent a rich man, untrained in diplomacy, unlearned in history and politics, who is a great publicity seeker and who is apparently ambitious to be the First Catholic President of the United States."[17]

Rose Kennedy arrived in London to join her husband in March of 1938 along with Kathleen and the six youngest children. Photographs and stories about their arrival made the front pages. The Kennedys moved into the 36-room ambassador's residence and were introduced to British society. Joe Kennedy remarked, "Rose, this is a helluva long way from East Boston." Bobby, who was 13, and six-year-old Ted, were enrolled in private schools in London while Eunice, Pat, and Jean attended convent schools. Rosemary was sent to a private

Kathleen, Robert, Ted, Pat, and Jean Kennedy depart for England in 1938 with their mother, Rose Kennedy. (John F. Kennedy Library)

On the embassy grounds in England in 1939: Eunice; John; Rosemary; Jean; Joe; Teddy; Rose; Joe, Jr.; Pat; Robert; and Kathleen Kennedy (Barbara Wilding)

school. Joe, Jr., and John were both at Harvard. John, who was fascinated by history, wrote his undergraduate thesis on England's position in World War II. (He later expanded it into a book called *Why England Slept*, which became a best-seller.) Joe graduated with honors and was elected a delegate to the Democratic National Convention in 1940. He wanted to become the first Irish-Catholic president of the United States.

Kathleen, 24, was working for the Red Cross. During this time she fell in love with William John Robert Hartington, the oldest son of the duke of Devonshire. Known as Billy Hartington, he was Protestant, and when he and Kathleen decided to marry their families could not agree on the terms of the wedding. Finally, the couple decided to have a civil ceremony in London. Rose and Joe were so upset that Kathleen was not being married in a Catholic church that they did not attend the ceremony. Only Joe, Jr., represented the Kennedys.

After graduating from Harvard, John Kennedy registered for the draft. He was number 18 chosen by his draft board, but he failed the physical and the army rejected him. He was determined, though, and undertook a fitness program, swimming regularly to get into shape. The navy was considered more "upper-class" than the army, and his father pulled strings to get him in. He joined in 1941 and was assigned to a desk job in the Office of Naval Intelligence several months before the Japanese attacked Pearl Harbor. When war broke out he was transferred to a training school and then to sea duty in the South Pacific as the captain of PT-109, a patrol torpedo boat. "I'm on my way to war . . . ," John wrote. "This job on these boats is really the great spot of the Navy."[18]

The PT boat, considered the "fighter plane of the sea," was swift and heavily armed but also flimsily constructed. In March 1943, while Kennedy's PT-109 was on night patrol in the Solomon Islands, the boat was rammed by a Japanese destroyer and cut in half. Two sailors were killed. The rest of the crew swam to a nearby island, with Kennedy towing a badly burned crew member, and they survived for seven days by eating coconuts and insects. At one point Kennedy swam out in search of help, without any luck. He then wrote a message on a coconut and handed it to a native. The message reached the navy, and the PT-109 crew was rescued. John received the Purple Heart and the Navy and Marine Corps Medal, and he kept the coconut on his desk for the rest of his life. His exploits as a heroic young naval officer were later detailed in an article in the *New Yorker* magazine.

Joe, Jr., was anxious to join the war, too, and he skipped his final year at Harvard Law School to enlist as a naval air cadet in 1941. He was stationed in Florida, Puerto Rico, and West Virginia, but he really wanted to get into the action. He volunteered for a dangerous aerial mission to destroy German rocket launchers positioned on the coast of France. "I am going to do something different for the next three weeks," he wrote to his parents on July 26. "It is secret and I am not allowed to say what it is, but it isn't dangerous so don't worry . . ."[19] On August 12, 1944, he piloted a navy PB4Y bomber carrying over 20,000 pounds of explosives and headed for his target. Without any warning, the plane exploded in midair with two tremendous blasts, killing him instantly.

Rose Kennedy wrote in her memoirs: "I ran upstairs and awakened Joe. I stood for a few moments with my mind half paralyzed. I tried to speak but stumbled over the words. Then I managed to blurt out that priests were here with that message. . . . We sat with the priests in a smaller room off the living room, and from what they told us we realized there could be no hope, and that our son was dead."[20]

Joe, Sr., was in shock; friends said that he would never be the same again. He retreated to his room at the house in Hyannis. Arthur Krock of the *New York Times*, a close friend of Kennedy's, recalled: "The death of Joe, Jr. was the first break in this circle of nine children, nearly all extraordinary in some way: handsome, intelligent, with a mother and father to whom they were devoted and who were devoted to them. It was one of the most severe shocks to the father that I've ever seen registered on a human being."[21] Joe was never able to talk of his son again without breaking down and crying. Two weeks later, there was more bad news. Kathleen's husband, Billy Hartington, had been killed by a sniper's bullet while in combat in Belgium. They had been married for just four months.

During these years, Robert Kennedy attended St. Paul's School in New Hampshire and Portsmouth Priory in Rhode Island and finished high school at Milton Academy in Massachusetts. He loved playing football, and even though he weighed just 150 pounds, he could tackle much larger players. "We were to try harder than anyone else," Robert Kennedy wrote. "We might not be the best, and none of us were, but we were to make the effort to be the best." Sam Adams, an old classmate, said, "He showed absolute determination; he decided to do something, he just gave it everything he had. . . . The things he was interested in, he did go all-out."[22] He neither smoked nor drank, and when he reached 21, he received a $2,000 bonus from his father. Six weeks before his 18th birthday, Robert enlisted in the Naval Reserve as an apprentice seaman while John began his political career. In 1945, the navy named a destroyer after Joe, Jr., and a year later, Robert F. Kennedy reported for duty on the *USS* Joseph P. Kennedy, Jr. He spent six months in the Caribbean, mostly scraping paint, and then received an honorable discharge. "The war was still fresh in people's minds down there," his shipmate Lem Billings recalled, "and they'd ask where we had been, what we'd done. Bobby didn't have anything to say. I used to kid him about it. He didn't think it especially funny."[23]

After her husband's death, Kathleen fell in love with another English Protestant, Peter Milton, Earl Fitzwilliam. He was married but intended to divorce his wife. Rose protested again; her daughter would be marrying a divorced man and a Protestant. On May 13, 1948, the couple boarded a small plane in France for a vacation in Cannes. They then planned to fly to Paris to meet Joe Kennedy, hoping to obtain his blessing. Although it was raining heavily, with fog and strong winds, they decided to fly anyway. The small, light plane was thrown against the mountains, and they were killed instantly. Joe Kennedy, who had traveled to France to meet them, identified his daughter's mangled body. "The sudden death of young Joe and Kathleen within a period of three years has left a mark on me that I find very difficult to erase," wrote Joe Kennedy to a friend.[24]

The ambitions that Joe Kennedy had held for his eldest son were passed on to John. "I got Jack into politics," he said. "I was the one. I told him Joe was deceased and that it was therefore his responsibility to run for Congress. He didn't want to. He felt he didn't have the ability and he still feels that way. But I told him he had to."[25]

"It was like being drafted," John said. "My father wanted his oldest in politics." In 1946, he began his campaign for a seat in the House of Representatives. He was just 28. Honey Fitz's old rival, James Michael Curley, had resigned from his seat in Congress to run for mayor of Boston, winning office in 1945. A special election was held for his vacant seat, with 17 candidates in contention. Every neighborhood in the 11th District was canvassed by a "Kennedy man." John Kennedy attended house parties and spoke of jobs, housing, medical care, and Social Security. He had looks, style, charisma, and charm. Joe Kennedy plotted strategy and spent a quarter of a million dollars buying ads and billboard space. Honey Fitz, then 83, campaigned as if *he* were the candidate, singing "Sweet Adeline" once again. Robert, just discharged from the navy, was assigned, reluctantly by his brother, to three Italian wards in East Cambridge. His wards went for another candidate, but by a smaller margin than had been expected. John Kennedy won by a landslide.

Robert enrolled at Harvard in 1944, majoring in government, playing football, and graduating in 1948. He served briefly as a foreign correspondent for the *Boston Post* when he was 22, traveling to Europe and the Middle East. His grades weren't good enough for Harvard Law School, so he enrolled at the University of Virginia Law School, where he graduated in 1951. He was 56th in a class of 124 with a grade point average of 2.54. One of his professors recalled, "He didn't volunteer much in class. He was a good, strong student . . . when you called upon him, he gave very good, sensible answers. He was a tough-minded sort of fellow, taciturn, and he didn't really sparkle very much."[26]

John Kennedy was reelected to Congress in 1948 but he wanted the Senate seat held by Henry Cabot Lodge, Jr. Lodge was the grandson of Henry Cabot Lodge, who had beaten Kennedy's grandfather, Honey Fitz, in a senatorial race in 1916. He had been in office since 1936. When John made his move in 1952, Robert managed his brother's campaign. "He's the only one who doesn't stick knives in my back, the only one I can count on when it comes down to it," commented John. In 1951, at 26, Bobby had joined the Department of Justice, working in Brooklyn, New York, as a $4,200-a-year government attorney investigating tax fraud, corruption, and bribery. His father wanted him to help his brother, but he liked what he was doing and was unfamiliar with Massachusetts politics. "I hate to leave such an interesting assignment as I have had in Brooklyn for the last three months. But I think I owe it to my brother John to return to Massachusetts and do my part before the Democratic primary in September," he said. "Of course, I think John is going to be the Democratic nominee and the new United States Senator from Massachusetts."[27] Robert organized the campaign as if his life depended on it, working 18-hour days. "Bobby could handle the father and no one else could have," said longtime Kennedy aide Kenneth O'Donnell. "Those of us who worked with him over the next few months are convinced that if Bobby had not arrived on the scene and taken charge when he did, Kennedy most certainly would have lost the election."[28] O'Donnell later recalled how Bobby utilized women campaign workers: "They'd leave leaflets on seats when they got off the bus, and toss them through the doors of taxicabs so that the next passenger would have something to read—nine hundred thousand copies of our folder—were distributed by hand. . . . We tried to telephone every voter in Massachusetts at least twice in that campaign."[29] Every member of the family campaigned with the slogan "Kennedy will do more for Massachusetts." His mother Rose, his sisters, and even his grandmother worked in the campaign, organizing 35 tea parties and entertaining over 75,000 women. His father had copies of the PT-109 story distributed to all registered voters. Opponents accused Kennedy of buying a congressional seat. John said to one, "I don't have to apologize for myself or any of the Kennedys. I'm running for Congress. Let's stick to that. If you want to talk about my family, I'll meet you outside."[30]

John Kennedy, the millionaire's son and war hero, won by 70,000 votes. He thanked his brother. "Until then," Lem Billings said, "I don't think Jack had been aware that Bobby had all this tremendous organizing ability. But during the campaign Bobby had proved himself again and again, forging a blood partnership that would last until the two of them died."[31] "Just as I went into politics because Joe died, if anything happened to me tomorrow, my brother Bobby would run for my seat in the Senate. And if Bobby died, Teddy would take over for him," said John.[32]

With John a senator poised to run for president, Joe Kennedy turned a critical eye on Robert. "You haven't been elected to anything. Are you going to sit on your tail end and do nothing now for the rest of your life? You'd better go out and get a job."[33]

Notes

1. John H. Davis, *The Kennedys: Dynasty and Disaster* (New York: McGraw-Hill, 1984), p. 45.
2. Rose Fitzgerald Kennedy, *Times to Remember* (Garden City, N.Y.: Doubleday, 1974), p. 135.
3. Kennedy, *Times to Remember*, p. 135.
4. *The Fruitful Bough: A Tribute to Joseph P. Kennedy*, privately printed by Ted Kennedy in 1965, p. 143.
5. Arthur Schlesinger, Jr., *A Thousand Days: John F. Kennedy in the White House* (Boston: Houghton Mifflin, 1965), pp. 79–80.
6. Davis, *The Kennedys*, p. 82.
7. Ronald Kessler, *The Sins of the Father: Joseph P. Kennedy and the Dynasty He Founded* (New York: Warner, 1996), p. 111.
8. Doris Kearns Goodwin, *The Fitzgeralds and the Kennedys: An American Saga* (New York: Simon & Schuster, 1987), p. 363.
9. Kessler, *Sins of the Father*, p. 43.
10. Kennedy, *Times to Remember*, p. 103.

11. Goodwin, *The Fitzgeralds and the Kennedys*, p. 363.
12. Arthur Schlesinger, Jr., *Robert Kennedy and His Times* (Boston: Houghton Mifflin, 1978), p. 33.
13. Jack Newfield, *Robert Kennedy: A Memoir* (New York: New American Library, 1969), pp. 41–42.
14. Goodwin, *The Fitzgeralds and the Kennedys*, p. 637.
15. Goodwin, *The Fitzgeralds and the Kennedys*, p. 428.
16. Davis, *The Kennedys*, p. 89.
17. Davis, *The Kennedys*, p. 94.
18. Davis, *The Kennedys*, p. 125.
19. Goodwin, *The Fitzgeralds and the Kennedys*, p. 686.
20. Kennedy, *Times to Remember*, p. 301.
21. Arthur Krock, *Memoirs: Sixty Years on the Firing Line* (New York: Funk & Wagnalls, 1968), p. 348.
22. Schlesinger, *Robert Kennedy and His Times*, p. 45.
23. William Manchester, *Portrait of a President* (Boston: Little, Brown, 1967), p. 21.
24. Richard Reeves, *President Kennedy: Profile of Power* (New York: Touchstone, 1994), p. 94.
25. *McCall's*, August 1957.
26. Ronald Goldfarb, *Perfect Villains, Imperfect Heroes* (New York: Random House, 1995), p. 4.
27. Victor Lasky, *Robert F. Kennedy: The Myth and the Man* (New York: Trident Press, 1968), p. 71.
28. Goodwin, *The Fitzgeralds and the Kennedys*, p. 762.
29. Ralph G. Martin, *A Hero for Our Time: An Intimate Story of the Kennedy Years* (New York: Macmillan, 1983), p. 51.
30. William Manchester, *Remembering Kennedy: One Brief Shining Moment* (Boston: Little, Brown, 1983), p. 38.
31. Goodwin, *The Fitzgeralds and the Kennedys*, p. 767.
32. Joe McCarthy, *The Remarkable Kennedys* (New York: Dial, 1960), p. 116.
33. Schlesinger, *Robert Kennedy and His Times*, p. 99.

3

THE KENNEDY TRADITION

Robert Kennedy was the first of the Kennedy sons to marry. He had been introduced to Ethel Skakel, who was a classmate of his sister Jean at Manhattanville College. One of six children, she was energetic, outgoing, and athletic; he was shy and serious. They were both religious and well-to-do. Skakel's father had founded Great Lakes Coal and Coke Company of Chicago. "I think they were very complementary because she was so outgoing," Jean Kennedy Smith recalled. "Well, he said that he was very much in love with Ethel and he'd like to marry her, and what did I think his chances were. And I said, 'Well, I'm not sure, because I know—I think Ethel might want to be a nun.' And he said, 'Well, I can compete up against anyone, but I can't compete against God.'"[1]

He later said that the best thing he ever did was to marry Ethel Skakel, which he did in 1950, when he was 24 and she was 22. Robert once sent her a note, quoting from the Bible: "And Ruth said: Entreat me not to leave Thee, or to return from following after Thee, for whither Thou goeth I will go; and where Thou lodgest I will lodge; Thy people shall be my people and Thy God my God. When Thou diest then I will die and we will be together forever." In 1957, the couple settled in Virginia in Hickory Hill, a large white mansion that had been built in 1810 and utilized as the headquarters of the Union Army during the Civil War. The white brick house sat on a hill surrounded by six acres. There was a tennis court

Robert Kennedy marries Ethel Skakel in 1950. (Stetner/John F. Kennedy Library)

and a pool in the back. Its previous occupants had been John Kennedy and his wife, Jacqueline Bouvier Kennedy, who were married in 1953. John, who had lost the vice-presidential nomination in 1956, decided to travel abroad with his father. While he was away, Jackie, then pregnant, suffered a miscarriage. She had too many painful memories of Hickory Hill, so they decided to sell the house to Robert and Ethel.

In 1957, the popular president Dwight D. Eisenhower was beginning his second term in office. The United States was strong and prosperous, but there were also fears of communism and of nuclear war. Diplomatic relations between the United States and the Soviet Union had been strained since 1917, when a revolution in Russia established a Communist government. After World War II, with the Soviet Union dominating most of Eastern Europe, the two superpowers embarked on what became known as the cold war. President Harry S Truman, who took office in 1945, had authorized the use of the atomic bomb against Japan, and the threat of nuclear war seemed very real, especially after the Soviets developed a nuclear bomb in 1949. The United States watched every move that the Soviet Union made, and the Soviets were equally wary of the United States. Each side thought the other wanted to rule the world, and each believed that its own political and economic system was superior to all others.

Within the United States, the threat of communism was exploited by J. Edgar Hoover and Senator Joseph McCarthy of Wisconsin. The FBI, under Director Hoover, had, since the 1920s, compiled information on groups and individuals that it felt were suspect. Beginning in 1950, Senator McCarthy gained prominence with his sensational and unsubstantiated claims of Communists in the government. McCarthy developed a huge following, and even his fellow senators were afraid to denounce him for fear of accusations against them. "There are today many Communists in America," he warned. "They are everywhere—in factories, offices, butcher shops, on street corners, in private businesses—and each carries with him the germs of death for society."[2]

In Birmingham, Alabama, all Communists were ordered to leave town. Professional wrestlers in Indiana were forced to sign loyalty oaths, while Ohio declared Communists ineligible for unemployment benefits. In Nebraska, each school district examined textbooks for foreign ideas, and several hours a week were set aside for the singing of patriotic songs. Tennessee ordered the death penalty for those seeking to overthrow the state government. Everyone—from entertainers to librarians to college professors—came under suspicion. People lost their jobs, even when there was no evidence to support the claim that they were Communists. In Hollywood, actors, actresses, directors, and screenwriters were investigated, and those suspected of being "red" were placed on a blacklist and not permitted to work. Supporters of McCarthy threatened to boycott movies, television shows, and radio programs and their sponsors if the blacklist was not enforced. Many careers were ruined, and some of the accused took their own lives. One suicide note read, "I have done nothing in my job which I did not think was in the best interests of this country. . . . When the dogs are set on you, everything you have done since the beginning of time is suspect."[3]

A friend of Joe Kennedy's, McCarthy had dated Pat Kennedy several times, and he visited the Kennedys' Hyannis home on occasion. Many of John Kennedy's constituents were supporters of McCarthy. A Kennedy aide once described McCarthy as "the *other* type of Irishman that Jack tried so hard to disassociate himself from." In December 1952, Joe Kennedy asked Senator McCarthy to appoint Robert Kennedy chief counsel of the Permanent Subcommittee on Investigations. But McCarthy had already decided to hire Roy Cohn, a 25-year-old lawyer who had already established a reputation as an anticommunist. Rather than offend Joe, McCarthy named Robert assistant general counsel.

Kennedy's major assignment was to determine the number of ships dealing with Communist China and to get Greek shipowners to stop dealing with Communist countries. Kennedy did not get along with Roy Cohn, who was similar in style to McCarthy. Cohn was considered intelligent, unpleasant, and vindictive. Kennedy resigned after six months, complaining that "most of the investigations were instituted on the basis of some preconceived notion by the chief counsel or his staff members and not on the basis of any information that had been developed. . . . I thought Senator McCarthy made a mistake in allowing the Committee to operate in such a fashion, told him so and resigned."[4] But Kennedy's relationship with Joe McCarthy would taint him for the rest of his life. Kennedy said that he would be entering private practice as a lawyer, which he never did. Instead, he joined the Hoover Commission, of which his father was a member, and worked on the commission's study of the federal government and bureaucracy. Kennedy served as assistant counsel

(1953–55) and as chief counsel (1955–57) of the Senate Permanent Subcommittee on Investigations. He served as chief counsel of the Senate Rackets Committee (1957–59), investigating the affairs of Teamsters union leaders Dave Beck and Jimmy Hoffa.

When Robert Kennedy later ran for senator in New York, his old connection with McCarthy was brought up. Because of it, many people never really trusted him. "At that time, I thought there was a serious internal security threat to the United States; I felt at that time that Joe McCarthy seemed to be the only one who was doing anything about it. I was wrong," he admitted.[5]

McCarthy's downfall came in 1954, when he accused the United States Army of "coddling communism" and was brought up on charges before the Senate. More than 20 million Americans watched the hearings on TV, and Ethel Kennedy attended each of the 36 sessions. The military showed that McCarthy and Cohn had sought favors for a former associate who had recently been inducted into the army. During the elections that year, the Republicans lost control of Congress to the Democrats, and McCarthy lost his position as chairman of the

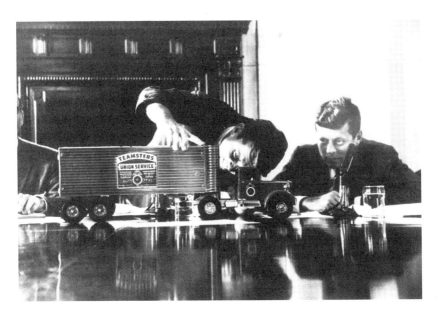

Robert Kennedy and Senator John Kennedy examine a Teamsters toy truck in 1957. (Look Photo Collection/John F. Kennedy Library)

Government Operations Committee and its Permanent Subcommittee on Investigations. The Senate voted to censure McCarthy. Cohn returned to private practice in New York. The era of McCarthyism was finally over. Although Kennedy thought that McCarthy could be cruel, he also thought that the Wisconsin senator really wanted to be liked. He remained on friendly terms with him—he asked McCarthy to be the godfather of his first child, Kathleen—and he attended McCarthy's funeral in 1957.

When John L. McClellan, a Democrat from Arkansas, became chairman of the investigations subcommittee, he named Robert Kennedy, 33, as chief counsel. Their first target was the Teamsters, the largest, richest, and most influential union in the United States. The union was made up of truckdrivers across the country and was headed by Dave Beck, whom Kennedy labeled a crook with a vast network of political and organized crime connections. Kennedy and his staff received thousands of letters from frightened workers about fixed elections, beatings, murders, and the illegal use of union funds. Kennedy dug through union records and discovered that the Teamsters had purchased Beck's home with $163,000 of union funds. No detail escaped him. He asked Beck during the Senate hearings, "Did you use union funds to purchase five dozen diapers for some of your friends at $9.68?" In response to Kennedy's interrogation, Beck invoked the Fifth Amendment 65 times. He was eventually convicted of larceny and tax evasion in 1959 and sentenced to five years in prison.

Kennedy, impatient, aggressive, direct, and abrasive, was called ruthless by some, but his father disagreed. "Bobby is soft—soft on people. All I ever meant to convey is that he had the capacity to be emotionally involved, to feel things deeply, as compared with Jack and that amazing detachment of his," remarked Joe Kennedy. "As a person who has had the term applied to him for fifty years, I know a little about it. Anybody who is controversial is considered ruthless. If he takes a stand against something, then he's called ruthless. It's ridiculous. Any man of action is always called ruthless."[6]

At one hearing, Kennedy and McClellan confronted Joey Glimco, the president of a Teamsters local in Chicago.

Robert Kennedy interrogates a witness at the McClellan hearings as Senator John Kennedy looks on, in 1957. (Look Photo Collection/John F. Kennedy Library)

KENNEDY: And you defraud the union?

GLIMCO: I respectfully decline to answer because I honestly believe my answer might tend to incriminate me.

KENNEDY: I would agree with you.

McCLELLAN: I believe it would.

KENNEDY: You haven't got the guts to [answer], have you, Mr. Glimco?

GLIMCO: I respectfully decline . . .

McCLELLAN: Morally you are kind of yellow inside, are you not?[7]

"My biggest problem as counsel is to keep my temper," Kennedy said. "I think we all feel that when a witness comes before the United States Senate he has an obligation to speak frankly and tell the truth. To see people sit in front of us and lie and evade makes me boil inside. But you can't lose your temper—if you do; the witness has gotten the best of you."[8] When a Teamsters lawyer called Kennedy a "vicious little monster," Kennedy was asked for a reaction. "Tell him I'm not so little," he replied.

When Beck was deposed as head of the Teamsters, Jimmy Hoffa replaced him. Kennedy began an investigation into Hoffa's activities at the end of January 1957 with a budget of $350,000 and 20 investigators and accountants. "Hoffa is evil," Kennedy said. "The Hoffas can destroy this country." In his book *The Enemy Within*, which was first published in 1959, he wrote that "by August of 1958, the McClellan Committee had uncovered a mass of crookedness and wrongdoing in the Teamsters. There were demands that Hoffa take steps to clean up his union. However, I was convinced by this time that he was completely incapable of doing the job—had he cared to. He was dependent on the racketeers and ex-convicts with whom he had surrounded himself. . . . This is a conspiracy of evil."9

Kennedy started his investigation of Hoffa by having dinner with him. "From what I've heard about you, maybe I should have worn my bulletproof vest," he said. Hoffa replied, "I only do to others what they do to me, only worse."10 Kennedy and his team went through ten file cabinets full of records and documents. Driving home one night, Kennedy noticed a light burning in Hoffa's office in the Teamsters building. He turned around and went back to work. The Teamsters spent over a million dollars to defend Hoffa during a 13-week trial featuring 114 witness and 15,000 government documents. "I made two disastrous mistakes in my life," Hoffa wrote in his autobiography. "The first was coming to grips with Robert F. Kennedy to the point where we became involved in what can only be called a blood feud. The result was that I became John F. Kennedy's steppingstone to the White House. And then the brothers Kennedy railroaded me to prison in March of 1967 and I spent four years and ten months in Lewisburg Penitentiary."11

Hoffa petitioned for a new trial, claiming government misconduct and attempting to get witnesses to change their stories. After three years of appeals, the U.S. Supreme Court upheld the conviction. Less than five years later, he was pardoned by President Richard Nixon. Hoffa disappeared in July 1975 and was presumed murdered.

By the end of Kennedy's four years with the Senate investigations committee, he and his staff had indicted 201 Teamsters officials and associates, winning 126 convictions. "The committee's investigations had shown that while the vast majority of Teamsters were honest, hard-working men, power had

Senator John Kennedy and Robert Kennedy in Washington, D.C., in June 1957 (Look Photo Collection/John F. Kennedy Library)

corrupted some of their leaders. Worse yet, the corruption was spreading," he wrote in his book *The Pursuit of Justice*. "Armed with great power and a vast treasury and guided by a philosophy that every man has his price, Mr. Hoffa and his henchmen used intimidation and violence and, finally, a desperate, massive assault on the jury system to retain their hold in the union. Finally, this year [May 1963] Mr. Hoffa and six associates were convicted of jury tampering in four different trials. Later, a jury which included eight union members found Mr. Hoffa guilty of defrauding the Teamsters Union pension fund of more than twenty million dollars—a cynical betrayal of the trust of working men and women."[12] Ethel Kennedy once said, "With Bobby, it's always the white hats and the black hats, the good guys versus the bad guys."[13]

Speaking at the American Society of Newspaper Editors' annual convention in April 1957, Kennedy said, "The Dave Becks of yesterday, the Jimmy Hoffas of today, will be forgotten. However, the defects in the law that permitted their operations will return to plague us with new Becks and Hoffas unless we find the basic solutions. The success or failure of this committee lies not in Dave Beck being denied the position of president emeritus of the Teamsters, or of Jimmy Hoffa

May 1960: Robert Kennedy campaigns before the primary in West Virginia.

under some half dozen federal indictments being elected president. It lies, rather, in our ability to arrive at solutions for problems that obviously exist, to develop the facts so that Congress will act."[14]

In 1960, John Kennedy, 42, announced his candidacy for the presidency. Robert resigned from the Justice Department to run his brother's campaign. Their first obstacle was to beat Hubert Humphrey, the senator from Minnesota, who was also running for the Democratic nomination. Kennedy won 56 percent of the vote in a Wisconsin primary that featured Humphrey traveling through the state via bus while the Kennedy family flew in a private plane. Kennedy purchased more time on television than Humphrey, who felt as if Kennedys were everywhere. By the time he reached the next primary in West Virginia, Humphrey was heavily in debt.

West Virginia was one of the toughest states to win. It was a poor state, with many coal miners out of work. The Kennedys saw hungry faces and deserted buildings. Protestants outnumbered Catholics, and West Virginia politics were considered corrupt and dirty. Polls showed Kennedy losing. There was talk that Joe Kennedy was buying votes. He was quoted as saying, "I will pay for a victory but I will not buy a landslide."[15] When

(Look Photo Collection/John F. Kennedy Library)

local politicians complained that Robert Kennedy was rude, he said, "It doesn't matter if I hurt your feelings. It doesn't matter if you hurt mine. The most important thing is to get the job done."[16] Kennedy won 61 percent of the vote and Humphrey took himself out of the running for president.

John Kennedy was nominated easily at the Democratic National Convention in Los Angeles, and he spoke of standing "on the edge of a New Frontier—a frontier of unknown opportunities and perils—a frontier of unfulfilled hopes and threats." Busy earning the Democratic nomination, Kennedy had not yet selected a vice president and had only 24 hours to choose one. He offered the position to Texas senator Lyndon Johnson, never thinking that Johnson would accept it. Robert did not want Johnson, and he tried unsuccessfully to get him to withdraw. Actually, Johnson was a sound choice politically, because he would bring in votes from the South.

John Kennedy's next opponent was Vice President Richard M. Nixon, the Republican nominee. Again the entire Kennedy clan became involved. Rose Kennedy and her daughters campaigned alongside John in front of exuberant, excited, and passionate crowds. Typically, John would be up before dawn, shaking as many as a thousand hands an hour. He promised to end segregation in public housing with "one stroke of a pen." When asked how he became a war hero, he replied, "They sank my boat." In September and October 1960, Kennedy and Nixon met in four historic debates that transformed both television and politics. Kennedy's image of youth, vigor, and style overshadowed the tense and distrustful countenance of Nixon. Kennedy was powerful and commanding, even though his critics complained that he was too rich, too Catholic, and had too much style and no substance.

Just before the election, civil rights leader Martin Luther King, Jr., participated in a sit-in at Rich's Department Store in Atlanta, Georgia, protesting segregated service. (Blacks were prohibited from eating at the lunch counter.) The protesters were arrested, and although charges were dropped against the others, King was held without bail. There was fear that King would be beaten or killed in jail, and his wife, Coretta Scott King, was deeply concerned for her husband's safety.

Senator Kennedy telephoned Mrs. King. "I want to express to you my concern about your husband. I know this must be very hard on you. I understand you are expecting a baby, and I just wanted you to know that I was thinking about you and Dr. King," he said. "If there's anything I can do to help, please feel free to call on me." Robert Kennedy called the judge who handled King's case and inquired about King's constitutional right to bail. The judge reluctantly agreed that King had a right to bail, and he was released. "They say that his call to me made the difference, that it elected him President. I like to think so. He was beginning to do so much, he and his brother," Coretta Scott King said.[17] This was the beginning of the Kennedys' involvement in civil rights.

On November 8, Election Day, the Kennedys gathered at Robert's house in Hyannis to await the election returns. Jacqueline Kennedy called it "the longest night in history."[18] The race was extremely tight, and Robert made phone calls until early morning checking the returns. Finally, Kennedy was declared the winner. He won the popular vote by only 119,450 out of 68.8 million votes cast, 49.7 percent to Nixon's 49.6 percent. John F. Kennedy became the youngest man ever elected president of the United States and the first Catholic. When he took the oath of office on January 20, 1961, he had fulfilled his brother Joe's destiny and his father's dream.

Notes

1. NBC, *Robert F. Kennedy: The Man and the Memories*, May 28, 1993.
2. David M. Oshinsky, *A Conspiracy So Immense: The World of Joe McCarthy* (New York: Free Press/Macmillan, 1983), p. 97.
3. Oshinsky, *A Conspiracy So Immense*, p. 271.
4. Arthur Schlesinger, Jr., *Robert Kennedy and His Times* (Boston: Houghton Mifflin, 1978), pp. 105–06.
5. Ronald Goldfarb, *Perfect Villains, Imperfect Heroes* (New York: Random House, 1995), pp. 4–5.
6. Lester David and Irene David, *Bobby Kennedy: The Making of a Folk Hero* (New York: Dodd, Mead, 1986), p. 111.
7. Ralph de Toledano, *RFK: The Man Who Would Be President* (New York: Signet, 1967), p. 95.
8. Schlesinger, *Robert Kennedy and His Times*, p. 150.
9. Robert F. Kennedy, *The Enemy Within* (New York: Harper & Row, 1963), p. 52.
10. Victor Lasky, *Robert F. Kennedy: The Myth and the Man* (New York: Trident Press, 1968), p. 104.

11. James Hoffa, *Hoffa: The Real Story* (New York: Stein and Day, 1976), p. 9.

12. Robert F. Kennedy, *The Pursuit of Justice* (New York: Harper & Row, 1964), p. 5.

13. William V. Shannon, *The Heir Apparent: Robert Kennedy and the Struggle for Power* (New York: Macmillan, 1967), p. 54.

14. Edwin O. Guthman and C. Richard Allen, *RFK: Collected Speeches* (New York: Viking, 1993), p. 45.

15. David Brinkley, *A Memoir* (New York: Knopf, 1995), p. 130.

16. Jack Newfield, *Robert Kennedy: A Memoir* (New York: New American Library, 1969), p. 28.

17. Harris Wofford, *Of Kennedys and Kings: Making Sense of the Sixties* (New York: Farrar, Straus & Giroux, 1980), p. 11.

18. William Manchester, *Remembering Kennedy: One Brief Shining Moment* (Boston: Little, Brown, 1983), p. 121.

4

ROBERT KENNEDY AS ATTORNEY GENERAL

"We're going to do what we thought Eisenhower was going to do in 1952 and never did—bring a new spirit to the government," Robert Kennedy said after his brother was elected president. "Not necessarily young men, but new men, who believe in a cause, who believe their jobs go on forever, not just from nine to five; who believe they have a responsibility to the United States, not just to an Administration, and who can really get things done. It really makes a hell of a difference."[1]

As John Kennedy was assembling his cabinet, his father said he felt that Robert was the best person for the job of attorney general. "I don't know what's wrong with Jack," Joe Kennedy said. "He needs all the good men he can get around him down there. There's none better than Bobby."[2] After four years of working for the Senate Rackets Committee, Robert wanted a different type of assignment. "I didn't want to be in the White House," he recalled. "I didn't want to do that. If I was going to be working in the government at all, I wanted to have a position of my own responsibility, not just taking direct orders from anybody. . . . I had to have a position which had equality of responsibility and prestige, because otherwise I would be resented, and rightfully so, by anybody for whom I would be working or anybody else who had a higher position. So I had to be in the Cabinet if I was going to perform that function," he said. "And the only place I could really be in the Cabinet was as Attorney General."[3] Just before announcing Robert's appointment as attorney general, John told his brother, "Damn it, Bobby, comb your hair." Robert recalled, "I brushed my hair and we went outside and announced it."[4] At the Senate confirmation hearings, only one person voted against his appointment. Senator Gordon Allott, a Republican from Colorado, said that Bobby Kennedy did not "have the legal experience to qualify him for the office."

Robert F. Kennedy, at 35, became the youngest attorney general in 150 years. His office oversaw the FBI and its director, J. Edgar Hoover, who was 66. For 30 years, the powerful Hoover had answered only to the president, bypassing the attorney general. Now he would have to answer to

Attorney General Robert Kennedy, FBI director J. Edgar Hoover, and President John Kennedy in May 1963 (John F. Kennedy Library)

young Robert Kennedy. Kenneth O'Donnell, a close aide of John Kennedy, recalled, "I knew Hoover wouldn't want him. He doesn't want the Attorney General to be more important than him."[5]

At the Justice Department, the youthful attorney general could be found sitting in his office with one foot on the top of his six-foot-square mahogany desk, in rolled-up shirtsleeves and loosened tie, sometimes shooting darts at a target on the wall. He often worked until nine or ten o'clock at night, and he expected others to do the same. He expected excellence and competence at every level and he was visible and accessible, often dropping into offices unannounced to introduce himself. "What's your name? What are you working on?" On his desk was a carved ivory monkey with the words "See no evil" and a copy of *The Enemy Within* in red leather binding, presented to him by Jacqueline Kennedy after the 1960 election. It was inscribed "To Bobby, who made the impossible possible and changed all our lives, Jackie" and "To Bobby, the brother within, who made the easy difficult, Jack, Christmas 1960."

Robert often brought his children and his dog to the office. By this time, he and Ethel had seven children. (There would eventually be 11.) Kathleen Hartington Kennedy, named after Robert's sister, was born in 1951, Joseph Patrick Kennedy III a year later, and Robert Francis Kennedy, Jr., in 1954. More Kennedys followed: David Anthony in 1955, Mary Courtney the following year, Michael LeMoyne in 1958, and Mary Kerry (later called just Kerry) in 1959. Later there was Christopher George in 1963, Matthew Maxwell Taylor in 1965, and Douglas Harriman in 1967. Robert taped their drawings to the walls of his office and added a comfortable sofa, a chin-up bar over the doorway, a stuffed Bengal tiger, and the family dog, Brumus. Hoover was horrified to see the Kennedy dog in the office and he complained. Kennedy stopped bringing the dog, but the children continued to be frequent visitors. Robert loved being a father, reading to his children when he came home at night and playing games with them. The children would "shave" with him in the morning, and at dinner he asked each child to summarize something from the news. "If I had a fight with one of my brothers or sisters, I would tell my father and he would tell me to get my brother. I would tell him my side of the story and my brother would have to sit in silence," recalled Kerry

At Hickory Hill in 1964: Robert; Ethel; Kathleen; Joseph; Robert, Jr.; David; Courtney; Michael; Kerry; and Christopher Kennedy (Look Photo Collection/John F. Kennedy Library)

Kennedy Cuomo. "And then my brother would tell his side of the story and I would be silent. He would make us kiss and make up and we'd go to our rooms and read for an hour. You need to get along with your brothers and sisters and the pursuit of knowledge is vital. That's a little memory but a very, very important lesson."[6]

The oldest sister, Kathleen Kennedy Townsend, remembered, "When he was home, the moments were very special, and not because they were relaxing—they were not—but because he challenged us. On Saturday mornings we had to practice before the touch football games. At dinner we were quizzed on history. At night we recited the rosary, and he read the Bible. . . . He taught his children that private happiness, or the happiness of one's own immediate family, was not enough. By his questions and by taking us to Senate hearings, to political rallies, to the playgrounds that he built for ghetto children, he taught each of us that participation in public affairs was worthy and honorable. And he made it an adventure, by challenging us to do well. . . . He was deeply religious. He believed in God, in good and evil, in virtue and sin, in truth and justice. He went to church and he meant it."[7]

"Before the children would go off to school, he always played twenty minutes to a half hour," recalled Ethel Kennedy. "They played football every morning, or at least threw the ball."[8] The Kennedy children spent the summers in Hyannis sailing, playing touch football and tennis, waterskiing, and sailing. Their father missed them keenly when they were away. "Sometimes," he said, "people think that because you have money and position you are immune from the human experience. But I can feel as lonesome and lost as the next man when I turn the key in the door and go into an empty house that is usually full of kids and dogs."[9]

Robert, John, and Ted Kennedy in Palm Beach in 1957 (Look Photo Collection/John F. Kennedy Library)

By January 1962, Robert was ranked as the second most powerful man in the Kennedy administration. Brother Ted made it a Kennedy trio in politics when he was elected to the Senate in 1962. Ethel Kennedy was the second most popular and visible woman in the country, next to her sister-in-law Jacqueline, who had refurbished the White House and promoted cultural activities on the Washington scene. Robert and Ethel hosted many parties and seminars at Hickory Hill. There was an air of fun and informality, with annual pet shows and guests—ranging from politicians and diplomats to football players, astronauts, writers, poets, and singers—who could never be certain if they were going to be tossed into the pool or not. Robert practically adopted the city of Washington, D.C., visiting schools, organizing sports and summer job programs, and hosting Christmas parties every year for poor children. He was spotted a few times with holes in the soles of his shoes. "Mother impressed on us the value of nickels, dimes and quarters," he said. "But we were never conscious of wealth. The opposite was preached constantly so we forgot about money. For example, I didn't bring any with me today. I just didn't think about it. He's the same way," he said of his brother.[10]

Kennedy often appeared without notice in Hoover's office, and he installed a buzzer in his office to summon him. The Kennedy children sometimes annoyed Hoover by pressing the buzzer. No one had ever treated Hoover this way before. He had a strict chain of command, but Kennedy would sometimes contact an FBI agent before he would contact Hoover. Kennedy assembled a sharp group of attorneys from law firms and law schools to work with him at the Department of Justice. Just two weeks into the Kennedy presidency, a radio newscaster reported that "the new Attorney General wants to go all out against the underworld. To do so, Bobby proposes a crack squad of racket busters, but J. Edgar Hoover objects. Hoover claims that a special crime bureau reflects on the FBI, and he is opposing his new boss."[11] Kennedy called for the establishment of a National Crime Commission. "The situation now is that the major figures of organized crime have become so rich and so powerful that they and their operations are in a large part beyond the reach of local officials," he said.[12] "The methods of our law-enforcement agencies have not kept pace with the improved techniques of today's criminals. We are still trying to fight the modern Al Capone with the weapons that we used twenty-five years ago. They are simply not effective."[13] Kennedy wanted the FBI to infiltrate organized crime syndicates. Hoover not only refused but he also denied the existence of the mob. The year before John Kennedy was elected president, only 35 mob figures were indicted, while in 1963, close to 300 mobsters were brought to trial. According to Robert Kennedy, "The FBI didn't know anything, really, about these people who were the major gangsters in the United States. That was rather a shock to me. . . . They took the position there wasn't any such thing as organized crime in the United States."[14] One FBI agent commented, "Bobby got the fight going again. He was a great and most capable guy."[15] "The gangsters of today work in a highly organized fashion and are far more powerful now than at any time in the history of the country," Kennedy wrote in *The Enemy Within*. "They control political figures and threaten whole communities. They have stretched their tentacles of corruption and fear into industries both large and small. They grow stronger every day."[16]

Secretary of State Dean Rusk, Vice President Lyndon Johnson, Attorney General Robert Kennedy, and President John Kennedy meet before Robert's trip around the world in February 1962. (John F. Kennedy Library)

Though he cared little about organized crime, Hoover had been keeping files on the Kennedy brothers (and other politicians) for years. "He's sending me stuff on my family and friends and even me, too," Robert Kennedy said. "Just so I know they are into all this information."[17] Hoover was considered dangerous as an enemy. "He's frightening . . . rather a psycho," Kennedy said.[18] Kennedy asked Hoover many times about the lack of blacks in the FBI. With the exception of a few secretaries, cleaning women, and maintenance men, there were only Hoover's chauffeur and a man who ran errands for him. None conducted investigations. "Oh, by the way, Edgar, how many blacks have you hired this month?" Kennedy asked, and ordered Hoover to hire more.[19]

In 1961, John Kennedy created the Peace Corps, a group of young, enthusiastic volunteers who would be assigned to work in various Third World countries. He was interested in the details of the space program and hoped to see the United States land astronauts on the moon before the end of the decade and before the Soviets did. Kennedy felt that he should cultivate smaller countries and their governments in order to keep communism from spreading. In February of 1962, he sent Robert and Ethel on a trip to Japan, Indonesia, Singapore, Vietnam, Taiwan, Hong Kong, Thailand, West Germany, Italy, the Netherlands, and France. They met with top officials and students in each country. "The United States is a nation dedicated to the emancipation of women, the education of children, and above all to the dignity of the individual," Robert Kennedy said in a speech at Nihon University in Tokyo. "This commitment to 'Life, Liberty and the Pursuit of Happiness' has inspired the essential motive of our national life: the unceasing search for new frontiers, not only frontiers of geography but also frontiers of science and technology and social and political invention and human freedom. These are the new frontiers which must be challenged and conquered by our generation—yours and mine."[20]

The first real test of the Kennedy administration was at the Bay of Pigs in Cuba. Before John Kennedy was elected, the Cuban dictator Fulgencio Batista, backed by the United States, had been overthrown by Fidel Castro, who soon instituted a Communist regime and became a dictator in his own right. Thousands of Cubans fled to Miami, and thousands more were imprisoned and executed by Castro. The U.S. Central Intelligence Agency (CIA) began, under President Eisenhower, to train Cuban exiles in Guatemala to fight Castro and his army. When Kennedy found out about these plans in 1961, he instructed CIA director Allen Dulles to continue with the project. According to the CIA plan, approximately 750 highly trained Cubans would invade Cuba by boat while air strikes eliminated Cuba's small air force. The Cuban Brigade would land on the south side of the island and their arrival would cause an uprising by the Cubans. The CIA wanted it to appear that the plan had been orchestrated by the Cubans, so that if it failed, the United States would not be blamed. When newspapers and magazines began reporting news of an impending attack, Kennedy assured the press and the public that the reports were unfounded. But a suspicious Castro mobilized over 200,000 of his soldiers throughout Cuba.

The Bay of Pigs invasion, launched on April 17, 1961, was a complete fiasco. The CIA reported that the Cuban air force had been wiped out, when actually only five planes had been destroyed. The 1,500 men of the Brigade arrived in boats and became stuck on coral reefs, which no one had been informed of. The men were trapped on the beach, and two of their boats were sunk, including one with radio and communications equipment. They had no way to communicate with each other. There was no uprising by the Cubans on the island. Over 100 members of the Brigade were killed and close to 1,200 captured. On December 24, the members of the Cuban Brigade who had been captured at the Bay of Pigs were returned to Florida in exchange for $53 million worth of drugs, medicines, and supplies. "How could I have been so far off base?" Kennedy asked. "All my life I've known better than to depend on the experts. How could I have been so stupid, to let them go ahead?"[21] President Kennedy took the blame for the disaster, organized a committee to investigate, and fired the director of the CIA. He brought his brother into meetings that concerned national security. But the damage was done, and the cold war between the United States and the Soviet Union intensified. A year and a half later, the cold war came close to being a nuclear war.

In 1962, satellite photos showed Soviet missile bases under construction in Cuba. Castro wanted the nuclear weapons in order to be taken seriously and to prevent an invasion by the United States. Robert Kennedy wrote in his book *Thirteen Days*, "The Russians were putting missiles in Cuba, and they had been shipping them there and beginning the construction of the sites at the same time those various private and public assurances were being forwarded by Chairman Khrushchev to President Kennedy. Thus the dominant feeling was one of shocked incredulity. We had been deceived by Khrushchev, but we had also fooled ourselves. No official within the government had ever suggested to President Kennedy that the Russian buildup in Cuba would include missiles."[22]

To deal with the crisis, President Kennedy gathered together a group of his closest confidants, forming the Executive Committee of the National Security Council (commonly called ExComm). Robert, his most trusted adviser, headed the committee. They faced difficult choices—should the United States act first and bomb the missile sites, which could mean the deaths of thousands of Cubans, or should they invade Cuba? If they hesitated and offensive missiles were fired from Cuba, over 8 million Americans could be dead within minutes. Worried children wrote letters to President Kennedy like the following:

Dear President,

I think we should use a water bomb to wash our enemys out.

—Thank you
Jimmy M

Dear Mr. President,

I am eleven years old and every night I worry. I worry about what will happen tomorrow, not so much as tomorrow, but as the future.

What will be left of this wonderful world in ten years if someone presses the button? What will be left of you and your family? All I'm asking for is PLEASE THINK before you press the button, please.

Sincerely yours
Roger N[23]

Robert Kennedy and Secretary of Defense Robert McNamara were in favor of a military blockade of Cuba. "Each one of us was being asked to make a recommendation which, if wrong and if accepted, could mean the destruction of the human race," Kennedy said.[24] The president and his committee voted 11 to 6 in favor of the blockade and against direct military action. On October 22, the president told the Soviet ambassador, Anatoly Dobrynin, that the blockade would be lifted only when the missiles were removed from Cuba. An hour later, in a nationally televised address, Kennedy explained, "The purpose of these bases can be none other than to provide a nuclear strike capability against the Western Hemisphere."[25] He said that he would use any means necessary to protect the United States and its citizens and that included nuclear war. Khrushchev sent a letter to Kennedy stating that the missiles were for defensive purposes only and that if the United States did not invade Cuba, the missiles would be removed. "We must not succumb to 'petty passions' or to 'transient things,'" Khrushchev wrote, "but should realize that if indeed war should break out, then it would not be in our power to stop it, for such is the logic of war. I have participated in two wars and know that war ends when it has rolled through cities and villages, everywhere sowing death and destruction. The United States," he continued, "should not be concerned about the missiles in Cuba; they would never be used to attack the United States and were there for defensive purposes only. You can be calm in this regard, that we are of sound mind and understand perfectly well that if we attack you, you will respond in the same way. But you too will receive the same that you hurl against us. And I think that you also understand this. . . . This indicates that we are normal people, that we correctly understand and correctly evaluate the situation. Consequently, how can we permit the incorrect actions which you ascribe to us? Only lunatics or suicides, who themselves want to perish and to destroy the whole world before they die, could do this. . . . We want something quite different . . . not to destroy your country . . . but despite our ideological differences, to compete peacefully, not by military means."[26]

Another letter arrived the following day. This time Khrushchev said that the Soviets would remove their missiles from Cuba only if the United States removed its missiles from Turkey. Robert

Kennedy suggested that his brother respond to the first letter and ignore the second. Kennedy wrote to Khrushchev on October 27, welcoming a prompt solution. He informed Khrushchev that if the missiles were not dismantled and if he did not receive a response in two or three days, then Cuba would be attacked. The strategy worked. On October 28, the Russians began to dismantle the Cuban missile sites. After 13 days of extreme international tension, the Cuban Missile Crisis was over.

However, conflict at home was escalating. Many people felt that there were two Americas—one for whites and one for blacks. In many parts of the South, schools, bus terminals, and housing were still segregated. Signs for restrooms and water fountains at airports and bus terminals read "Colored" and "Whites Only." Blacks could not eat in the same restaurants as whites, nor could they lodge in the same hotels. Blacks were forced to sit in the back rows on buses and in movie theatres. Southern churches were segregated, and blacks were not allowed to use public libraries or swim in public pools. They could not get quality education or health care. Blacks were ordered to call white men "Mister." A black man could be arrested and even lynched for looking at a white woman, and blacks had to step off the sidewalk to make room for passing whites. Innocent men were arrested, beaten, and jailed for crimes they did not commit. And most white lawyers would not take civil rights cases.

Before the passage of the Voting Rights Act of 1965, which prohibited voting discrimination, very few blacks in the South were registered to vote. Various methods, including literacy and character tests, harassment, threats of physical violence, and payoffs, obstructed black registration. "An integral part of all this is that we make a total effort to guarantee the ballot to every American of voting age—in the North as well as in the South. The right to vote is the easiest of all rights to grant," said Robert Kennedy. "The spirit of our democracy, the letter of our Constitution and our laws require that there be no further delay in the achievement of full freedom to vote for all. Our system depends upon the fullest participation of all its citizens."[27]

The Kennedys did not have a clear civil rights program at first, but rapidly moving events forced them to grapple with the issue. A month after John Kennedy was elected in 1960, four black college students sat down at a whites-only lunch counter at Woolworth's in Greensboro, North Carolina, and requested service. They were told to leave, but they refused to move. Within three days, they had been joined by dozens of other students, black and white. The Greensboro protesters were cursed and spat upon but they continued their sit-in until July 25, when the lunch counter agreed to serve blacks. Other sit-ins and protests at various other stores followed around the state.

John Kennedy took a cautious approach to civil rights, because he was dependent on southern Democrats to get his legislative program passed in Congress. But Robert soon adopted a more aggressive approach at the Justice Department. John Doar, an assistant in the Civil Rights Division of the Justice Department, commented: "He was always wanting to move, get something done, accomplish something, and when I first went up to see him—probably April 1961—he was for filing seventy-five cases by Thanksgiving."[28]

On May 4, 1961, the Freedom Rides began as a group of blacks and whites prepared to challenge segregation laws in seating assignments, restrooms, and terminals. (A Supreme Court ruling in December 1960 had declared segregation illegal on trains and buses and in terminals, but southern officials had ignored the ruling.) The Freedom Riders left Washington, D.C. in two buses, bound for Alabama and Mississippi. On May 15, one bus was burned and vandalized in South Carolina. Five days later, the second group was attacked in Montgomery, Alabama. Mobs threw rocks and bottles, and police refused to intervene. Robert Kennedy sent in 400 federal marshals trained in riot control along with his administrative assistant, John Siegenthaler. When Siegenthaler tried to help two young girls being menaced by a mob, he was hit from behind and knocked unconscious. At this point Kennedy wanted state and local police to act, but the governor would not even return his telephone calls. Only after President Kennedy intervened did the governor promise to protect the Riders en route from Montgomery to Jackson, Mississippi. But then the Greyhound Bus Company could not find any drivers. Robert Kennedy called the company and told them that "the government is going to be very upset if this group does not get to continue their trip, [so] somebody better get in the damn bus and get it going and get these people on their way."[29] A driver was found, and the Freedom Rides continued. Robert Kennedy then called Senator James Eastland of Mississippi, who guaranteed the safety of the Freedom Riders in his state. Though 300 were arrested, there was no violence. At this point Kennedy petitioned the Interstate Commerce Commission to end segregation of interstate buses and terminals. In September 1961, the order was issued and signs for "White" and "Colored" disappeared from the terminals.

Birmingham, Alabama, was one of the most segregated cities in the country, and on April 2, 1962, Martin Luther King, Jr., organized a protest against discrimination at lunch counters and department stores there. King, who preached nonviolence and mobilized churches in the civil rights movement, was arrested by police commissioner Bull Connor after leading a protest march, and he was not allowed to contact anyone. When Coretta Scott King could not reach her husband, she telephoned the White House. Robert Kennedy returned her call

Meeting with civil rights leaders in the Rose Garden in June 1963 (John F. Kennedy Library)

and promised to look into the situation. The president called her the following day to say that Reverend King was fine and would call her. King was released on bond after eight days. He then organized over 2,000 men, women, and children to march in protest of discrimination. Snarling police dogs lunged at children as police officers aiming high-powered water hoses knocked the protesters off their feet. The rest of the country watched these events unfold on television. As the protests continued, city officials reached a settlement with civil rights leaders, agreeing to desegregate stores and businesses. When this pact was threatened by mob violence, the Kennedys settled the issue by threatening to send in 3,000 federal troops. "This government will do whatever must be done to preserve order, to protect the lives of its citizens, and to uphold the law of the land," President Kennedy said. "The fires of frustration and discord are burning in every city . . . where legal remedies are not at hand."[30]

In September 1962, James Meredith confronted the South's segregated educational system when he applied to the University of Mississippi. "Ole Miss," as it was called, had been all white for over 100 years. Eight years earlier, the Supreme Court had ruled in *Brown v. Board of Education* that public schools had to be desegregated, but the process was moving very slowly. Meredith, who had served nine years in the U.S. Air Force and attended all-black Jackson State College, filed suit in federal court for admission to Ole Miss. The Supreme Court declared him eligible to enroll, but his entrance was blocked by Mississippi governor Ross Barnett, who insisted that no black would be a student at Ole Miss. Robert Kennedy took charge of the case and struck a deal with Barnett. Barnett promised he would allow Meredith to attend the school after some initial token public resistance to please his constituents. Kennedy agreed to give Barnett some leeway, as long as the governor promised to keep order on the campus. But when Meredith attempted to register, Barnett physically barred his way, and a mob surrounded the building, shouting, "Go home, nigger!" Men lined up outside carrying shotguns and rifles, and a tense stand off ensued. After more than 20 conversations with Kennedy over several days, Barnett agreed to withdraw if federal marshals took over. But thousands of white demonstrators assaulted the marshals with bricks, rocks, bottles, and guns as they escorted Meredith in to register. Two innocent bystanders were killed, 28 people suffered gunshot wounds, and 206 marshals were injured. "The idea that we got through the evening without the marshals being killed and without Meredith being killed was a miracle," said Robert Kennedy.[31] President Kennedy went on national television on September 30, urging peaceful desegregation of the school. "If this country should ever reach the point where any man or group of men by force or threat could long defy the commands of our court and our Constitution," he said, "then no law would stand free from doubt, no judge would be sure of his writ, and no citizen would be safe from his neighbors." By October 1, over 2,000 federal troops occupied Oxford, Mississippi. Meredith enrolled; Ole Miss was finally desegregated.

"The events in Birmingham and elsewhere have so increased the cries for equality that no city or state or legislative body can prudently choose to ignore them," President Kennedy said. "It is a time to act in Congress." In mid-1963, the Kennedy administration proposed to extend the life of the Civil Rights Commission for four years, fortify voting rights, and give the attorney general more authority in school desegregation cases. In order to gain perspective, Robert Kennedy wanted to speak with blacks directly to find out what they were feeling. On May 24, 1963, he gathered a group that included author James Baldwin, singers Harry Belafonte and Lena Horne, psychologist Kenneth B. Clark, and playwright Lorraine Hansberry. He listened to their expressions of frustration, but the participants felt that they were really not getting through. "This was one of the most anguishing experiences I've ever had," said Clark. "If this was the best white America had to offer, then God help us. . . . There was real lack of communication. It was macabre." "They don't know anything," Kennedy said in his own defense. "They don't know what the laws are—they don't know what the facts are—they don't know what we've been doing or what we're trying to do. . . . It was all emotion, hysteria. They stood up and orated. They cursed. Some of them wept and walked out of the room."[32] But the meeting affected him, and he remembered it for the rest of his life.

On June 11, 1963, Medgar Evers, the Mississippi state director of the National Association for the Advancement of Colored People (NAACP), was shot to death as he stepped out of his car in his driveway. That summer, 33 black churches were bombed. On August 28, 1963, Martin Luther King, Jr. led a March for Jobs and Freedom in Washington, D.C. The Kennedy brothers were against the march at first and tried to talk King out of it. But when they saw that the march was going to take place whether they liked it or not, they endorsed it. A multiracial crowd estimated at almost half a million heard King's famous speech: "I have a dream that one day this nation will rise up and live out the true meaning of its creed—we hold these truths to be self-evident, that all men are created equal. . . . When we allow freedom to ring, when we let it ring from every village and hamlet, from every state and every city, we will be able to speed up that day when all of God's children—black men and white men, Jews and Gentiles, Protestants and Catholics—will be able to join hands and sing in the words of the old Negro spiritual. 'Free at last, free at last; thank God almighty, we are free at last.'"[33]

While the Kennedys were pushing for civil rights reforms at home, they confronted a growing crisis in Vietnam, which had been divided since 1954. The United States supported the government of Ngo Dinh Diem in South Vietnam and backed Diem against threats from Communist North Vietnam and from the Vietcong—antigovernment guerrilla fighters based in the South. President Kennedy sent military advisers to Vietnam, and by 1962, there were 12,000 American troops there. In February 1962, Robert Kennedy traveled to Southeast Asia and vowed, "We are going to win in Vietnam. We will remain here until we do win." He added, "The American people will see Vietnam through these times of trouble to a period when the Vietnamese people will find a long-sought opportunity to develop their country in peace, dignity and freedom."[34] But the situation in Vietnam continued to deteriorate. President Kennedy told one of his aides before he left for Dallas, Texas, on November 21, 1963, "When you get back, after the first of the year, I want you to organize an in-depth study of every possible option we've got in Vietnam, including how to get out of there. We have to review this whole thing from the bottom to the top."[35]

President Kennedy traveled to Dallas to mend political fences and to gather support for his coming reelection campaign. "I know nothing can happen to him. I tell you, something's watching out for him," Joe Kennedy once said. "I've stood by his deathbed four times. Each time I said good-by to him, and he always came back. . . . When you've been through something like that back, and the Pacific, what can hurt you? Who's going to scare you?"[36]

But on November 20, when Robert Kennedy turned 38, Ethel Kennedy remarked to a friend, "It's all going too perfectly."[37] Two days later, John and Jacqueline Kennedy entered Dealey Plaza in Dallas in an open-top blue Lincoln convertible. They sat in the back seat while Texas governor John Connally and his wife Nellie sat in the front. As they waved and smiled at the crowds, Lee Harvey Oswald, a 24-year-old ex-marine, fired a rifle from the Texas School Book Depository. Jacqueline Kennedy shouted, "My God, what are they doing? My God, they've killed Jack, they've killed my husband."

J. Edgar Hoover telephoned Robert, who was home at Hickory Hill, and gave him the shattering news. Bobby hung up the telephone. "Jack's been shot!" he said with a look of horror on his face. At 1:00 P.M., President Kennedy was pronounced dead at Parkland Memorial Hospital. He was 46. He had served for two years, ten months, and two days—one thousand days filled with a sense of excitement and hope. Robert stayed in Washington to take care of the details of the funeral. His younger brother, Ted, was sent to Hyannis to comfort their parents. Rose already knew. Joe, who had suffered a stroke in 1961, was paralyzed on one side and unable to speak. But he understood. Columnist James Reston wrote in the *New York Times*: "America wept tonight, not alone for its dead young president, but for itself. The grief was general for somehow the worst in the nation had prevailed over the best. The indictment extended beyond the assassin, for something in the nation itself, some strain of madness and violence, had destroyed the highest symbol of law and order."[38]

Robert Kennedy never thought that his brother would be the target for assassination, for it was he, Robert, who had gone after Hoffa and the mob. "There's so much bitterness. I thought they'd get one of us," he said, right after the event. "I thought it would be me." Robert met Air Force One in Washington, D.C., when it arrived with his brother's body. Mrs. Kennedy was still wearing her bloodstained suit. A friend heard Robert sob and cry out, "Why, God?"[39] In a letter to his oldest son, Joe, he

Robert and Ted Kennedy, with Jacqueline Kennedy, lead the funeral procession of John F. Kennedy to Arlington National Cemetery. (John F. Kennedy Library)

wrote, "Remember all the things that Jack started—be kind to others that are less fortunate than we—and love our country. Love to you—Daddy."[40]

In the following days Kennedy lost weight; his face was gaunt and lined, his eyes puffy. He hardly slept. At the funeral, he took off his PT-109 tie pin and placed it in the coffin along with an engraved silver rosary that Ethel had given him at their wedding. Now the head of the Kennedy clan, he comforted his sister-in-law and her children, Caroline and John.

He took long walks by himself, frequently visiting his brother's grave with its eternal flame at Arlington National Cemetery. On each anniversary of the assassination, he spent time in prayer and seclusion. "All of November is a bad time for him," said one of his friends.[41] He often awakened in the middle of the night at Hickory Hill, and would drive his convertible in mid-winter with the top down. "You couldn't get to him," Ethel Kennedy said. "It was too deep. You know, it's like somebody's had a terrible shock to their system, and it—it's in them. It has to come from inside."[42] He would work late at the Justice Department, and in the evening he would stand or pray quietly at his brother's grave. "When Jack died, a large part of Bobby died, too," said family friend Lem Billings. "I saw that life extinguished. He had tied up so much of his own self, his own career, to that of his brother. He had been totally involved, totally dedicated to helping and furthering the work of John Kennedy. Hitching himself so completely to Jack, he established no identity of his own and never wanted one. So when they buried Jack Kennedy in that grave at Arlington, they buried much of Bobby, too."[43]

"No wonder, then, that Bobby at first acted as if he had been cut adrift and did not know quite what to try to do in the years ahead," Rose Kennedy wrote. She observed in her diary, "Bobby is here, but seems to be distracted by the confusion and uncertainty surrounding his own plans. He feels that he should do nothing to prevent his being chosen by President Johnson to run as Vice-President [in 1964], although he thinks it unlikely that will happen. Sometimes he talks about going abroad for a year to write a book or just to get away from it all."[44]

He continued as attorney general in the Johnson administration, his office filled with memorabilia of his brother. He and Lyndon Johnson had a dislike for each other that dated back to 1960. Kennedy thought that Johnson was a liar, and Johnson called him an upstart. Kennedy never forgot that the day after his brother was killed, Johnson was behind his brother's desk in the Oval Office. Less than three months after John Kennedy was assassinated, Johnson asked Robert Kennedy to review the funeral bills. The two man also differed philosophically. Johnson thought that federal programs were the answer to public problems, while Kennedy did not believe that they were. Kennedy was confrontational and passionate; Johnson was a dealmaker and was at his best negotiating settlements.

Kennedy considered running for governor of Massachusetts but was afraid that he and his brother Ted would have to compete with each other. He volunteered to become the United States ambassador to South Vietnam, but President Johnson felt that it was too dangerous. Johnson was running for reelection in 1964, and Kennedy thought the best position for him would be as vice president because Johnson had pledged to carry out his brother's policies. He hoped that Johnson would ask him to run, even though he had misgivings. "I'm just trying to make up my mind what I'm going to do", he said. "I think it's a great problem, of course, if I stayed as Vice President and was forced on him. It would be an unpleasant relationship, number one. Number two, I would lose all ability to ever take any independent positions on matters."[45]

Johnson recalled in his book *Vantage Point*, "My relationship with Bobby Kennedy from the earliest hours of my Presidency—and before that, as far back as the 1960 campaign—had usually been cordial, though never overly warm. John Kennedy and I had achieved real friendship. I doubt his younger brother and I would have arrived at genuine friendship if we had worked together for a lifetime. Too much separated us—too much history, too many differences in temperament." Johnson called Kennedy into his office the evening before the Democratic National Convention and told him that he would not be considered because the Republican senator Barry Goldwater of Arizona had entered the race for president. "I have concluded, for a number of reasons, that it would be inadvisable for you to be the Democratic candidate for Vice President in this year's election. . . . The nomination of Senator [Barry] Goldwater is the decisive factor in reaching the conclusion that I have reached. Goldwater's strength will be in the South, the Southwest and possibly in the Middle West; also it is my belief that the Border States will be of unusual importance in this particular election," he said. "If Goldwater runs a strong race, it is entirely possible that the outcome of the election could rest in the Middle West."[46]

Based on that strategy, Johnson chose Senator Hubert Humphrey of Minnesota as his running mate. Kennedy appeared at the Democratic National Convention to introduce a film about his brother. He looked and sounded so much like John that many at the convention were moved to tears, and he received a standing ovation. "I realize that as individuals, and even more important, as a political party and as a country, we can't just look into the past, we must look to the future," he told the delegates. "If we do our duty, if we meet our responsibilities and our obligations, not just as Democrats, but as American citizens in our local cities and towns and farms and our states and in the country as a whole, then this generation of Americans is going to be the best generation in the history of mankind. . . . When I think of President Kennedy, I think of what Shakespeare said in Romeo and Juliet: 'When he shall die take him and cut him into stars and he shall make the face of heaven so fine that all the world will be in love with night and pay no worship to the garish sun.'"[47]

Johnson beat Barry Goldwater for president by over 16 million votes. However, the mood of the United States began to unravel with the escalation of the Vietnam War; less than a month after he was sworn in, Johnson added more American troops to the war effort, trying to stave off a Communist victory. Kennedy pondered his future and decided to run for senator from New York. "I began to think about it a lot, continuously in fact, after [John] died, as a means to continue what he and I had begun together," he said. "You see, not the President alone, but we all were involved in certain tasks and certain dreams he wanted to translate into reality. Then, all of a sudden, he was no longer there to do it. I understood that it was up to me to carry them forward, and I decided to do so."[48]

Notes

1. *Newsweek*, November 21, 1960.
2. Doris Kearns Goodwin, *The Fitzgeralds and the Kennedys: An American Saga* (New York: Simon & Schuster, 1987), p. 807.
3. Edwin O. Guthman and Jeffrey Shulman, *Robert Kennedy in His Own Words* (New York: Bantam, 1988), p. 74.
4. Harris Wofford, *Of Kennedys and Kings: Making Sense of the Sixties* (New York: Farrar, Straus & Giroux, 1980), p. 92.
5. Anthony Summers, *The Secret Life of J. Edgar Hoover* (New York: Putnam, 1993), p. 320.
6. Interview with the author, November 1996.
7. *People*, June 6, 1988.
8. NBC, *Robert F. Kennedy: The Man and the Memories*, May 28, 1993.
9. William vanden Heuvel and Milton Gwirtzman, *On His Own: RFK 1964–68* (Garden City, N.Y.: Doubleday & Co., 1970), p. 179.
10. William Manchester, *Portrait of a President* (Boston: Little, Brown, 1962), p. 98.
11. Summers, *The Secret Life of J. Edgar Hoover*, p. 326.
12. Speech, Associated Press Managing Editors meeting, Dallas, Texas, November 15, 1961.

13. Robert F. Kennedy, *The Enemy Within* (New York: Harper & Row, 1963), pp. 263–64.
14. Guthman and Shulman, *Robert Kennedy in His Own Words*, p. 120.
15. Summers, *The Secret Life of J. Edgar Hoover*, p. 328.
16. Kennedy, *The Enemy Within*, p. 229.
17. Richard Reeves, *President Kennedy: Profile of Power* (New York: Touchstone, 1994), p. 288.
18. Reeves, *President Kennedy*, p. 66.
19. Summers, *The Secret Life of J. Edgar Hoover*, p. 63.
20. Edwin O. Guthman and C. Richard Allen, *RFK: Collected Speeches* (New York: Viking, 1993), p. 75.
21. Theodore C. Sorenson, *The Kennedy Legacy* (New York: Macmillan, 1969), p. 309.
22. Robert F. Kennedy, *Thirteen Days* (New York: Norton, 1969), pp. 27–28.
23. Bill Adler, *Kids' Letters to President Kennedy* (New York: Morrow, 1963), pp. 69, 138.
24. Kennedy, *Thirteen Days*, p. 44.
25. Arthur Schlesinger, Jr., *Robert Kennedy and His Times* (Boston: Houghton Mifflin, 1978), p. 808.
26. Kennedy, *Thirteen Days*, p. 87.
27. Speech, University of Georgia Law School, Atlanta, Ga., May 6, 1961.
28. Victor S. Navasky, *Kennedy Justice* (New York: Atheneum, 1971), p. 96.
29. Wofford, *Of Kennedys and Kings*, p. 153.
30. William Manchester, *Remembering Kennedy: One Brief Shining Moment* (Boston: Little, Brown, 1983), p. 237.
31. Guthman and Shulman, *Robert Kennedy in His Own Words*, p. 165.
32. Victor Lasky, *Robert F. Kennedy: The Myth and the Man* (New York: Trident, 1968), p. 188.
33. Irving Bernstein, *Promises Kept: John F. Kennedy's New Frontier* (New York: Oxford University Press, 1991), pp. 116–17.
34. *New York Times*, February 19, 1962.
35. Reeves, *President Kennedy*, p. 66.
36. William Manchester, *Portrait of a President* (Boston: Little, Brown & Co., 1962), p. 237.
37. Manchester, *The Death of a President*, p. 33.
38. James Reston, *Deadline* (New York: Random House, 1991), p. 292.
39. Wofford, *Of Kennedys and Kings*, pp. 411–12.
40. Schlesinger, *Robert Kennedy and His Times*, p. 612.

41. Jack Newfield, *Robert Kennedy: A Memoir* (New York: New American Library, 1969), p. 30.
42. NBC, *Robert F. Kennedy: The Man and the Memories*, May 28, 1993.
43. Lester David and Irene David, *Bobby Kennedy: The Making of a Folk Hero* (New York: Dodd, Mead, 1986), p. 221.
44. Rose Fitzgerald Kennedy, *Times to Remember* (Garden City, N.Y.: Doubleday, 1974), p. 457.
45. Guthman and Shulman, *Robert Kennedy in His Own Words*, p. 414.
46. Lyndon Baines Johnson, *The Vantage Point* (New York: Holt, Rinehart & Winston, 1971), p. 99.
47. Wofford, *Of Kennedys and Kings*, p. 419.
48. Vanden Heuvel and Gwirtzman, *On His Own*, p. 6.

5

SENATOR FROM NEW YORK

Now 38, Robert F. Kennedy resigned as attorney general and decided to run for the Senate, representing New York against the incumbent senator, Frank Keating. Critics complained that Kennedy was running as the ghost of his brother, that he was not a resident of the state and had no business there. "I would not have entered this campaign unless my candidacy had conformed to the laws of the State of New York and the Constitution of the United States," he said at the New York State Democratic Convention on August 12, 1964. "And despite what has been written and said my candidacy establishes no precedent. There have been many similar cases around the country and even here in New York. . . . Further, for every citizen who is a New Yorker by birth there is one who is a New Yorker by choice, or whose parents were. I am in the second category." He and his mother gave speeches and teas during the campaign, and they worked out a little routine. "Tell them, Mother," Robert would say. Rose would then speak of moving from Brookline to Bronxville when Robert was two and would say that he had attended schools in New York for years and that her husband's business interests were in New York. "You know," Robert said to a crowd of potential voters, "my brother Jack and I never wanted to appear on a platform with her, because she's the real campaigner. She's been campaigning for something like seventy-two years. . . . Was it for Grover Cleveland's Administration or maybe Lincoln's that you began, Mother?" he teased. He spent approximately $1 million on a campaign that featured him in television campaign ads saying, "Strange as it may seem, I just want to be a good United States Senator." His campaign theme was "Let's put Bob Kennedy to work for New York." Wherever Kennedy campaigned, he was mobbed, whether it was in New York City or Long Island or in upstate New York. Voters ignored the fact that he was not from New York, even though he could not vote for himself. Because of his association with Joe McCarthy and his reputation for being ruthless, liberal voters were hesitant to vote for him, but Kennedy won by more than 700,000 votes. "We started something in 1960," he said in his victory statement, "and the vote today is an overwhelming mandate to continue." He thanked his campaign workers by quoting from Alfred, Lord Tennyson's poem "Ulysses": "Come my friends, 'Tis not too late to seek a newer world."[1]

Robert and Ted Kennedy (reelected to his brother's old seat in Massachusetts) were sworn in together as senators on January 5, 1965. They served together on the Labor and Public Welfare Committee, and Robert was also on the Government Operations and District of Columbia Committees. "Politically, [the Kennedys] were all quite different," wrote the journalist James Reston years later. "Joe was even more conservative than his father. Jack was a moderate. Robert was in motion, running away from his liaison with Senator Joe McCarthy on the right toward center. Edward was an unabashed liberal, even when in the eighties the Republicans tried to give that distinguished tradition a bad name."[2]

Robert Kennedy placed a plaque next to the door of his Senate office, quoting former president Theodore Roosevelt: "It is not the critic who counts. The credit belongs to the man who is actually in the arena—whose face is marred by dust and sweat and blood, who at the best knows in the end the triumph of high achievement and who at the worst if he fails at least fails while daring greatly so that his place will never be with those cold and timid souls who know neither victory nor defeat."

Jeff Greenfield, an ABC News correspondent and political commentator, worked for Kennedy as a legislative aide from 1967 through 1968. "He demanded that you think about stuff more than anyone else, whether it was a speech or a legislative program. He had an unbelievable knack for asking the question that you forgot to ask or hadn't bothered to ask. He wasn't content with the first blush answer," Greenfield recalled. "The first day I was in his office he had me tag along with him to a hearing regarding Federal education monies. 'Don't tell me you solved the problem because you spent money. Are the kids learning? Are people benefitting? What's going on?' The most important aspect was watching the way he worked."[3]

Kennedy spoke of his brother's legacy at the University of Rochester in Rochester, New York, on September 29, 1964. "If John F. Kennedy's life stood for anything, it was for the fact that an individual can make a difference—that an individual has an obligation and a responsibility to try to make a difference. I think that whether in the field of civil rights or in the field of housing, the problems that are facing us in Latin America or Asia or Berlin or any of these places, all of us must make some kind of sacrifice—make some kind of effort—on behalf of our country, and on behalf of our own fellow citizens, and on behalf of the citizens of the world—it is absolutely essential."[4]

A month after Kennedy entered the Senate, the United States began its first air strikes over North Vietnam. By the end of July, President Johnson announced that he was sending 50,000 more men to Vietnam. The bombing missions fueled the antiwar movement: students demonstrated at college campuses around the country; many burned their draft cards, and some fled to Canada to avoid military service. By 1966, 350,000 American troops were in Vietnam and the war was on television every night. George Skakel, a nephew of Ethel Kennedy, was killed in Vietnam. Villages were being destroyed by napalm and soldiers were returning home in body bags. Johnson declared that the United States was winning, but television images and photographs of the war told a different story.

Kennedy became a passionate opponent of the war in Vietnam, speaking at college campuses across the country, where he was much in demand. He was not afraid to be challenged, welcoming confrontation and listening to differing opinions. He spoke at Marymount College in upstate New York in December 1967: "Do you know what that means, when you ask for more bombing? It means you are voting to send people, Americans and Vietnamese, to die. . . . Don't you understand that what we are doing to the Vietnamese is not very different than what Hitler did to the Jews?"[5]

Kennedy believed that Johnson's Vietnam policies were ripping the United States apart. Speaking to an audience following the publication of his book *To Seek a Newer World*, he said, "For the sake of those Americans who are fighting today, if for no other reason, the time has come to take a new look at the war in Vietnam; not by cursing the past but by using it to illuminate the future. And the first and necessary step is to face the facts. It is to seek out the austere and painful reality of Vietnam, freed from wishful thinking, false hopes and sentimental dreams. . . . We will find no guide to the future in Vietnam unless we are bold enough to confront the grim anguish, the reality of that battlefield which was once a nation called South Vietnam, stripped of deceptive illusions. It is time for the truth."[6]

Kennedy also became an advocate for the poor, who up until that time had been largely invisible to politicians and to the general public. He was shocked and appalled at how some Americans were living, and he was determined to publicize their needs. "The poor, in this America, are usually poor precisely because they are without education, without knowledge, without the means to take advantage of what help we can offer," he said.[7] In another speech he asserted, "The problem of poverty is the problem of the youth, whether they 'hang around' at the side of a muddy road in West Virginia or on a street corner in Harlem. They can be found, differing only in number, in every city and hamlet in the United States."[8] He believed that concerned citizens could make a difference: "The future does not belong to those who are content with today, apathetic toward common problems and their fellow man alike, timid and fearful in the face of new ideas and bold projects. Rather it will belong to those who can blend passion, reason and courage in a personal commitment to the ideas and great enterprises of American society."[9]

Kennedy also championed the rights of blacks, Hispanics, migrant workers, and American Indians.

Twenty million Negro Americans, five million Mexican-Americans, nearly three million Puerto Ricans, and half a million Indians are a reality. The slums are a reality, as are idleness and poverty, lack of education and dilapidated housing. Frustrated expectations and disappointed hopes are a reality. Above all, the awareness of injustice and the passion to end it are inescapable realities. Thus, we can face our difficulties and strive to overcome them, with imagination and dedication, wisdom and courage. Or we can turn away—bringing repression, steadily increasing human pain and civil strife, and leaving a problem of far more terrible and threatening proportions to our children.[10]

In April 1967, Kennedy visited the Mississippi Delta, where blacks lived in shacks without electricity or running water. Machines had replaced workers in the fields. Going from shack to shack, he touched children with swollen bellies who were dying of hunger. Many had never visited a doctor or a dentist. Kennedy was outraged. Food stamps cost two dollars a person for families whose income was under thirty dollars a month. "I've seen bad things in West Virginia," he said, "but I've never seen anything like this anywhere in the United States."[11] Kennedy told Orville Freeman, the secretary of agriculture, "Orville, get the food there." Because of Kennedy, Freeman lowered the cost of food stamps to fifty cents, and saw to it that eggs, fruit juice, and other nutrients were added to the surplus food program. Because of Kennedy's involvement, other senators made hunger an issue.

Recognizing the complaints and the resentment of the black community, Kennedy said: "It is difficult to live in the shadow of a multimillion-dollar freeway, to watch the white faces blur as they speed by the problems of the city, returning each evening to the pleasant green lawns of the suburbs. And it must be difficult beyond measure to share in America's affluence enough to own a television set—and to see on that set the hate and fear and ugliness of little Negro children being beaten and clubbed by hoodlums and thugs in Mississippi."[12] He wanted to reform the welfare system and felt that people were not only short on money but short on self-esteem. "We have spent more and more money on welfare; but will we be ready to admit that welfare has also destroyed self-respect and encouraged family disintegration—will we be ready instead to do what we must to bring its recipients into full participation in our society?" he asked.[13] "In the long run, welfare payments solve nothing, for the givers or the recipients; free Americans deserve the chance to be fully self-supporting—and this requires education."[14]

Kennedy believed that jobs were the answer to many problems and called for a welfare system based on need, with national standards and incentives for people to work. "If we are to deal most directly with the deficiencies in our social programs, we will place the highest priority on making sure men have jobs. For there is no real alternative. . . . Welfare workers, or higher welfare payments, cannot confer self-respect or self-confidence in men without work: in the United States, you are what you do," he wrote.[15]

As head of the President's Committee on Juvenile Delinquency and Youth Crime, Kennedy organized a campaign to keep potential dropouts in school and persuaded Congress to give over $600,000 for a youth program. When the administration allocated $327,000,000 for Head Start programs for deprived children for their first school year, Kennedy objected that the funds would cover only 30 percent of the children who needed it. "It's a point that distresses me. We're spending more than $300,000,000 on a supersonic jet transport that will eventually cost $4 billion. But we can't help 210,000 more children. I just can't be content with that. It's an outrage."[16] He fought for schools and playgrounds in Washington, D.C., and he walked the streets of Harlem. Only July 2, 1964, President Johnson signed the Civil Rights Act of 1964, prohibiting discrimination on the basis of color, race, religion, or national origin. A month later, the Criminal Justice Act, which Kennedy spearheaded, became law. His committee reported that there were two different systems of criminal justice—one for the rich, the other for the poor. Thousands of poor people who were put in jail were kept there for weeks or months because they could not afford bail. The Criminal Justice Act stated that defendants in federal court must be provided with paid legal counsel if they could not afford it themselves.

Kennedy traveled to Germany in 1964 to commemorate his brother's trip to Berlin shortly before he had been assassinated. "There were so many who felt that a light had been snuffed out, that the torchbearer for a whole generation was gone," he said. "But I have come to understand that the hope President Kennedy kindled is not dead, but alive. . . . The torch still burns, and because it does, there remains for all of us the chance to

Senator Robert Kennedy and Cesar Chavez on the day Chavez broke a 25-day fast, March 1968 (Archives of Labor and Urban Affairs, Wayne State University)

light up the tomorrows and to brighten the future. For me, that is the challenge that makes life worthwhile."[17]

In early 1966, the Senate migratory labor subcommittee, of which Kennedy was a member, held hearings in Delano, California, regarding tactics used against labor leader Cesar Chavez and his organizers. Chavez had formed the Farm Workers Association in 1962, teaching migrant workers how to read English and manage their money. These men and women followed the crops, traveling from farm to farm. The hours were long, the wages were low, and the work in the fields was very difficult. Children worked beside their parents; only a few went to school. Housing camps were small and cramped, with as many as 12 people living in one bedroom. Sometimes there was no running water. Chavez organized several strikes in 1966 on some of the large grape farms. He demanded higher wages and recognition for his organization. In response, the farm owners hired replacement workers. The strikers picketed, and the local sheriff arrested 44 strikers and photographed them—in order, he said, to identify potential troublemakers. The sheriff explained to Kennedy that the replacement workers told him, "'if you don't get [the pickets] out of here, we're going to cut their hearts out.' So rather than let them get cut, we removed the cause." Kennedy replied angrily, "[Can] I suggest during the luncheon period that the sheriff and district attorney read the Constitution of the United States?"[18] Kennedy urged Chavez's followers to aim for "a patient, careful building of a democratic organization. Along that road lies success. Along that road lies the building of community, solidarity and brotherhood, the building of institutions and cooperative businesses, of clinics and schools and homes. . . . You are winning a special kind of American citizenship. No one is doing it for you—you are winning it for yourselves. And, therefore, no one can ever take it away."[19]

"I think Senator Kennedy had incredible courage and compassion," said union leader Dolores Huerta. "He associated with the very poor. He told the sheriff to read the Constitution. He was arresting the strikers. It was a very dramatic moment. He had that way of just connecting." Kennedy investigated and found that the Labor Department and Immigration allowed large farms to hire strikebreakers from Mexico, failing to enforce the law that forbade entry permits to workers heading to farms involved in labor disputes. Kennedy made a strong protest to the government, and when he returned to Washington he began looking into conditions in other areas. Kennedy took field trips to migrant labor camps, including one in upstate New York, where he found migrants living in fly-infested shacks, abandoned buses, and in one case, a chicken coop. He helped to bring farm workers under the protection of the laws permitting collective bargaining and outlawing child labor. He sought to raise the minimum wage for migrants and increase the number of workers the law protected.

Meanwhile, the rage of the black community was reaching a boiling point. When blacks rioted in the Watts section of Los Angeles in 1965, stores were looted and set afire, with entire blocks gutted. Thirty-four people died and more than a thousand were injured. Kennedy observed, "We say to the young, stay in school—learn and study and sacrifice—and you will be rewarded the rest of your life. But a Negro youth who finished high school is more likely to be unemployed than a white youth who drops out of school and is more likely to find only menial work at lower pay. One leader of the Watts riot was a biochemistry graduate. We should not be surprised."[20] A week later, he spoke at a convention in New York. "I want to speak with you tonight about some of the events of the last week: about the dead and the orphans of the rioting in Los Angeles; about the sick and the distressed of all our urban ghettos; about the hatred and the fear and the brutality we saw in Los Angeles; and about what we can and must do if this cancer is not to spread beyond control. . . . For it is clear that the riots of the last weekend were no isolated phenomenon, no unlucky chance. They began with a random argument between a drunken driver and a policeman; they could as easily have begun with a fight in a dance hall, as did the riots in Rochester; or with a policeman shooting a boy armed with a knife, as did the riots in New York; or with a fire engine knocking over a lamppost and killing a pedestrian, as did the riots in Chicago. . . . All these places—Harlem, Watts, South Side—are riots waiting to happen."[21]

Regarding the plight of the American Indian ("our first citizen"), Kennedy wrote in *The Pursuit of Justice* that the life expectancy of the American Indian was "forty-two years, twenty years less than for Americans as a whole." American Indians were the poorest of Americans, with incomes 75 percent below the national average and unemployment rates ten times the national average. They were dying of tuberculosis and alcoholism. Kennedy became the chairman of a study of Indian education.

Kennedy traveled to Peru, Chile, Brazil, Argentina, and Venezuela on a three-week tour as part of the Alliance for Progress, a ten-year plan for political, economic, and social development in Latin America begun by John Kennedy. He was greeted by "VIVA KENNEDY" signs in Peru, where he told students that "the responsibility of our times is nothing less than a revolution." He also traveled to South Africa, still drastically segregated by apartheid, and was mobbed both by white students in Johannesburg and by black crowds in the township of Soweto. A newspaper said that "Senator Robert

Kennedy's visit is the best thing that has happened to South Africa for years. It is as if a window has been flung open and a gust of fresh air has swept into a room in which the atmosphere had become stale and fetid." In an article for *Look* magazine, Kennedy called South Africa "a land of sadness, humanity hiding behind color." Speaking at Cape Town University, he said, "We must recognize the full human equality of all our people—before God, before the law, and in the councils of government. . . . We must do it for the single and fundamental reason that it is the right thing to do. . . . Each time a man stands up for an ideal or acts to improve the lot of others or strikes out against injustice, he sends forth a tiny ripple of hope, and crossing each other from a million different centers of energy and daring, those ripples build a current that can sweep down the mightiest walls of oppression and resistance."[22]

"Bobby gave people hope," said Ethel Kennedy. "One fellow there said the greatest thing that could have happened was knowing that someone in the United States cared. That has remained such a vivid memory for me."[23]

Robert Kennedy gave speeches at conventions, bar associations, rotary clubs, and chambers of commerce, but he spoke

Robert Kennedy during a Senate campaign tour   (Bill Eppridge, *Life* magazine, © Time Inc.)

more on college campuses than anywhere else. When he was booed at a campus he told the audience, "I know that's not the popular attitude, but it happens to be the way I feel about it. . . . You say, 'Tell it like it is' and tell you the truth and that's what I intend to do." His speeches were noted for their directness, passion, lack of political rhetoric, and relevance. "There is discrimination in New York, apartheid in South Africa and serfdom in the mountains of Peru. People starve in the streets of India; intellectuals go to jail in Russia; thousands [of Communists] are slaughtered in Indonesia; wealth is lavished on armaments everywhere. These are differing evils. But they are the common works of man," he said on one occasion.[24] He wrote his speeches on ruled legal paper with a pen or pencil; his handwriting was small, cramped, and difficult to read. He often read in the evening and he carried a book with him while he traveled, underlining passages for later reference. He listened to Shakespeare as he shaved in the mornings. One of his aides said of his speeches that "you have to understand he got to where he couldn't make it come out of his throat if he didn't believe it. He would literally lie awake at night, thinking about all the people in all of those places around the country—the world, really—depending on him, and he took so seriously his responsibility for making things better for them."[25]

In a speech to students at the University of California at Berkeley, Kennedy said, "The future does not belong to those who are content with today, apathetic toward common problems and their fellow man alike, timid and fearful in the face of new ideas and bold projects. Rather it will belong to those who can blend passion, reason and courage in a personal commitment to the ideals and great enterprises of American society. It will belong to those who see that wisdom can only emerge from the clash of contending views, the passionate expression of deep and hostile beliefs."[26]

In 1966, Kennedy turned his attention to the Bedford-Stuyvesant section of Brooklyn, New York, the second-largest black ghetto in the country, with almost half a million people living within five square miles. Brownstones were in a state of disrepair, and empty lots were strewn with garbage and old car parts. Many businesses had closed or moved out of the area. There was only one high school and no hospital. Eighty percent of teenagers from Bedford-Stuyvesant were high

Senator Robert Kennedy at the Bedford-Stuyvesant Restoration Corporation,
1967 (The Bedford-Stuyvesant Restoration Corporation)

school dropouts. Twenty-eight percent of families had incomes
of less than $3,000 a year, and Bedford-Stuyvesant received
almost no federal aid. "We got in touch with Bobby Kennedy to
tour Bedford-Stuyvesant," recalled Elsie Richardson, who ac-
companied him through the neighborhood. "After the tour he
said that he thinks he'll have a study done. My response was
we've been studied to death so let's come with brick and
mortar."[27]

And he did. Bedford-Stuyvesant became Kennedy's private
war on poverty. With support from the city of New York, grants
from foundations, and technical help from universities in
Brooklyn, he and Jacob Javits, the senior senator from New
York, sponsored an amendment to the poverty bill that provided $45 million in funds for job training and economic devel-
opment. Kennedy launched the Bedford-Stuyvesant
Restoration Project with an initial federal commitment of $7

million for two years. "To turn promise into performance, plan into reality," he said, "we must combine the best of community action with the best of the private enterprise system. Neither by itself is enough; but in their combination lies our hope for the future. . . . For this is a task of unparalleled difficulty. This is not just a question of making Bedford-Stuyvesant 'as good as' someplace else. We are striking out in new directions, on new courses, sometimes perhaps without map or compass to guide us. We are going to try, as few have tried before, not just to have programs like others have, but to create new kinds of systems for education and health and employment and housing. . . . We here are going to see, in fact, whether the city and its people, with the cooperation of government and private business and foundations, can meet the challenges of urban life in the last third of the twentieth century."[28]

The day after Kennedy announced his proposal for Bedford-Stuyvesant, he presented a broader version designed for other inner-city neighborhoods. "But I would concentrate now on my proposal for the ghetto," he said. "It begins with a base of employment, in a vastly expanded and accelerated program of urban reconstruction. Our cities are in dire need of rebuilding. . . . Our needs, and the programs we will now undertake to meet them, are in fact an opportunity to make every government program, and many private efforts, more effective than ever before. . . . The heart of the program, I believe, should be the creation of Community Development Corporations, which would carry out the work of construction, the hiring and training of workers, the provision of services, the encouragement of associated enterprises."[29] He sponsored the Model Cities Act and the Economic Opportunity Act, which established community development corporations. Community development corporations, in Kennedy's plan, would initially be financed by the federal government. Then CDCs would receive the same funds as any other nonprofit housing corporation. The bulk of funds would come from loans. The Bedford-Stuyvesant Restoration Project, it was hoped, would create jobs, improve housing, sanitation, and health care conditions, and help make the community self-sufficient. Kennedy lined up the heads of major corporations such as IBM and CBS, and also enlisted former secretary of the treasury Douglas Dillon. The Restoration Corporation was divided into two boards, one made up of community leaders and the other of business leaders. The business leaders, who were white, wealthy, and influential, were headed by André Meyer, the head of international banking at the investment firm of Lazard Frères. The board of community members, who were black, was led by Thomas Jones, a civil court judge. As the Restoration's first project, the Sheffield Farms bottling plant building was rebuilt by neighborhood workers. It was in a large abandoned section on Fulton Street that symbolized the decay and hopelessness of Bedford-Stuyvesant, and it was used as headquarters for the Restoration Project and its network of community services. IBM built a plant and employed 300 people from the neighborhood. In 1968, *Newsweek* called the project "the most sweeping and comprehensive rehabilitation effort ever brought to bear on a single American community." Kennedy personally attended every board meeting. He said, "If I could do what I really wanted to do, I would resign from the Senate and run Bedford-Stuyvesant."[30]

As a result of these efforts, blacks saw Kennedy as a man who could change things. He brought them hope. "This cannot continue," Kennedy insisted. "It must not continue. For all around our nation, Negroes and Puerto Ricans, Mexican-Americans and Indians, poor whites in Appalachia and in blighted inner-city areas, are waking up to what we have. They are demanding their rights as human beings."[31] During the summer of 1967, riots broke out in Detroit, New York, Newark, Buffalo, Atlanta, and other cities. Kennedy insisted, "Violence isn't the answer. Violence won't get you better housing or better jobs or better education for your children. The way to change things is by voting for change." He said, "We meet at a time [when] our nation is on the brink of its greatest domestic crisis since the Civil War. . . .[This] violence is not simply an aimless outburst of savagery, nor the product of outside agitators. It is brutal evidence of our failure to deal with the crisis in urban America and of our failure to bridge the widening gap between the affluent and the poor, black and white Americans."[32]

Kennedy spoke of dreams and hope to the crowds that gathered to hear him. "What is required of us is that we do more than recite those accomplishments and talk of dreams fulfilled," he said. "For now we must be prepared to work a revolution at once as profound and as compassionate as the struggle of the past thirty years. The question is whether we have lifted our eyes to the new horizons of our days, and to the uncharted oceans beyond. The question is whether we are prepared to dare—whether we will risk our positions and our popularity, our intellectual and social comforts in order to make a world for our children which is truly better than the world our fathers passed on to us."[33]

Notes

1. Arthur Schlesinger, Jr., *Robert Kennedy and His Times* (Boston: Houghton, Mifflin, 1978), p. 676.
2. James Reston, *Deadline* (New York: Random House, 1991), p. 297.
3. Interview with the author, December 1996.
4. Douglas Ross, *Robert F. Kennedy: Apostle of Change* (New York: Pocket Books, 1968), p. 9.
5. Jack Newfield, *Robert Kennedy: A Memoir* (New York: New American Library, 1969), p. 140.
6. Jules Witcover, *Eighty-five Days: The Last Campaign of Robert Kennedy* (New York: Morrow, 1969), p. 48.
7. Address, Albert Einstein College of Medicine, Yeshiva University, New York, March 18, 1965.
8. Address, Lexington Democratic Club, New York, February 4, 1965.
9. Speech, University of California at Berkeley, Berkeley, Calif., 1966.
10. Robert F. Kennedy, *To Seek a Newer World* (Garden City, N.Y.: Doubleday, 1967), p. 20.
11. Nick Kotz, *Let Them Eat Promises: The Politics of Hunger in America* (Englewood Cliffs, N.J.: Prentice-Hall, 1969), p. 2.
12. Speech, University of California at Berkeley, October 22, 1966.
13. Address, Retail, Wholesale and Department Store Union Convention, Miami Beach, Fl., May 27, 1966.
14. Speech on behalf of Democratic candidates for state office, Detroit, Mich., October 29, 1966.
15. Victor Lasky, *Robert F. Kennedy: The Myth and the Man* (New York: Trident, 1968), p. 34.
16. Lasky, *Robert F. Kennedy*, p. 324.
17. William vanden Heuvel and Milton Gwirtzman, *On His Own: RFK 1964–68* (Garden City, N.Y.: Doubleday, 1970), p. 385.
18. Schlesinger, *Robert Kennedy and His Times*, p. 791.
19. Vanden Heuvel and Gwirtzman, *On His Own*, p. 105.
20. Vanden Heuvel and Gwirtzman, *On His Own*, p. 81.

21. State Convention, Independent Order of Odd Fellows, Spring Valley, N.Y., August 18, 1965.

22. Address, Cape Town University, Cape Town, South Africa, June 6, 1966.

23. *Ladies' Home Journal*, February 1991.

24. Kennedy, *To Seek a Newer World*, p. 289.

25. Edwin O. Guthman and Jeffrey Shulman, *Robert Kennedy in His Own Words* (New York: Bantam, 1988), p. 5.

26. Speech, University of California at Berkeley, October 22, 1966.

27. Interview with the author, October 1996.

28. Speech, Brooklyn, N.Y., December 10, 1966.

29. Statement, Subcommittee on Executive Reorganization of the Senate Committee on Government Operations, December 10, 1966.

30. Vanden Heuvel and Gwirtzman, *On His Own*, p. 94.

31. Address, Day Care Council of New York, New York, May 8, 1967.

32. Testimony, National Commission on Urban Problems, New York, September 6, 1967.

33. Address, Retail, Wholesale and Department Store Union Convention, Miami Beach, Fl., May 27, 1966.

6

PROMISE FOR THE FUTURE

As the Vietnam War became an increasingly divisive issue, Robert Kennedy spoke out more frequently against U.S. policy in Southeast Asia. In *To Seek a Newer World*, he wrote, "We cannot remake South Vietnamese society, or ask the South Vietnamese people to give their national allegiance to the United States. . . . This is a war for the allegiance of the people. If after thirteen years of American involvement, and over two years of major combat participation, the 'other war' has failed to attract the allegiance of the people of Vietnam, we must ask ourselves whether all the sacrifice—the scars which will still be borne twenty and more years from now by today's Vietnamese children and American young men—will have been for the benefit of forgotten generals and a selfish elite. . . . There is the national interest, and there is also human anguish. To protect the one and prevent the other, there is no effort too great for us to make."[1]

Kennedy believed that the war served no purpose. "It became unmistakably clear to me that as long as Lyndon B. Johnson was President, our Vietnam policy would consist of only more war, more troops, more killing, and more senseless destruction of the country we were supposedly there to save," he said.[2] In January 1967, Kennedy spent an hour with the president of France, General Charles de Gaulle, who told him, "You are a young man with a brilliant future that will affect both your country and the world. I am an old man," he said, "who has lived through many battles and bears many scars, so listen closely to what I say to you: Do not become embroiled in this difficulty in Vietnam. Then you can survive its outcome. Those who are involved will be badly hurt. When their effectiveness is destroyed, you will be able to step in at the proper time, and help your country regain its proper course."[3]

Presidential elections were to be held in 1968, and Kennedy received thousands of letters, telegrams, and telephone calls urging him to run. He was constantly asked what his plans were. "I can't plan, I don't even know if I'll be alive in 1972," he said. "Fate is so fickle."[4]

Robert and Ethel Kennedy discussed the possibility of his running. He thought of his brother John and of Dallas. Ted Kennedy did not want to see Robert enter the race for the presidency. "I was against him running," he said. "I just had the concerns about the whole issues of safety. And I—I just had an unease about the race."[5] Robert's sister-in-law Jacqueline tried to talk him out of it; she was certain that someone would kill him. "You know, if I'm ever elected President," he told an aide, "I'm never going to ride in one of the goddamn bubble top cars."

In March 1968, Cesar Chavez fasted to dramatize the farm-workers' struggle against grape owners in California, and when he agreed to end his fast after 25 days, he invited Kennedy to join him in the mass at Thanksgiving. "That was a very big thing for us," recalled Dolores Huerta. "I had met him once before and I didn't think that he would recognize me. That shocked me. I asked him if he would come to see Cesar. Politicians are usually flaky. He didn't hesitate. I was so excited. People didn't believe me. He did come. In those days we were struggling for credibility. People didn't believe us. It was going to bring us to the attention of the world. Everyone was yelling for him to become President. That's when he decided to run. There were thousands of people. It was a mob scene. Everyone wanted to be close to him. Never once did he say 'let me out of here.' He took all the fingers and hands that reached out to him."[6]

At the mass, Kennedy shared communion bread with Chavez and called him "a hero for our times." He said, "And that's why I come here today to honor Cesar Chavez, for what he's done and what he stands for. How desperately you, and the people of this country—of our country—need him today. I come here today to honor you for the long and patient commitment you have made for this struggle for justice. And I come here to say that we will fight together to achieve for you the aspirations of every American: decent wages, decent housing, decent school-ing, a chance for yourselves and your children. You stand for justice and I am proud to stand with you."[7]

Kennedy announced his candidacy for the presidency of the United States on Saturday, March 16, 1968, in the Senate Caucus Room, the same room where his brother had an-nounced his own candidacy eight years earlier. (Both brothers were 42 when they became candidates.) Kennedy wore a gold PT-109 tie clasp in honor of his brother. "I do not run for the Presidency merely to oppose any man but to propose new policies," he said. "I run because I am convinced that this country is on a perilous course and because I have such strong feelings about what must be done that I am obliged to do all I can. . . . I run because it is now unmistakably clear that we can change these disastrous, divisive policies only by changing the men who make them. For the reality of recent events in Vietnam has been glossed over with illusions. The report of the Riot Commission has been largely ignored. The crisis in gold, the crisis in our cities, the crises on our farms and in our ghettos, all have been met with too little and too late. . . . In these next eight months we are going to decide what this country will stand for—and what kind of men we are. So I ask for your help, in the cities and homes of this state, into the towns and farms, contributing your concern and action, warn-ing of the danger of what we are doing, and the promise of what we can do in the future . . . not just in Southeast Asia, but here at home as well, so that we might have a new birth for this country, a new light to guide us," he said. "And I pledge to you, if you will give me your help, if you will give me your hand, I will work for you, and we will have a new America."[8]

As a candidate, Kennedy was a year and a half behind schedule. He had only 12 weeks to organize his effort in six primaries. His wife, Ethel, pregnant with their 11th child, his mother, and almost every family member worked in the cam-paign. The Democratic primaries began on May 7 in Indiana and would end in New York on June 18 as Kennedy's campaign began to shape up. His brother Ted became his closest adviser, while his brother-in-law, Steve Smith, managed the campaign. Kennedy worked 16-hour days traveling across the country, winning four out of five primaries in the first 80 days. He appealed to a wide cross-section of the electorate, including college students, the poor, the working class, blacks, and Hispanics. As he exited his plane, people would knock over police barricades, yelling, "Bobby! Bobby! Bobby!" They grabbed at his hands, his hair, and his clothes. He often lost his cuff links, and once someone even took his shoes. Students held up signs at colleges: I LOVE BOBBY. BOBBY IS GROOVY. SOCK IT TO 'EM BOBBY. He promised "a rebirth of the national soul" and an end to the Vietnam War and to racial discrimination. He promised jobs and higher wages and better living conditions. He believed that individuals could make a difference.

Kennedy quickly moved ahead of President Johnson in public opinion polls. Then, on March 31, 1968, Johnson made a dramatic and shocking announcement: "I shall not seek and I will not accept the nomination of my party for another term as your President." Senator Eugene McCarthy of Minnesota (no relation to Senator Joe McCarthy) and Vice President Humphrey each announced their candidacy for the Democratic nomination.

One of Kennedy's first stops along the campaign trail was Indiana, where he arrived for a month of campaigning, riding through the state on the Wabash Cannonball train. He always ended his speeches with a quote from George Bernard Shaw: "Some men see things as they are and ask why. I dream things that never were, and ask why not?" It became the signal to the reporters traveling with him that the train was about to move on. On April 4, just after he boarded his plane for Indianapolis to speak to residents of a black neighborhood, Kennedy received word that Martin Luther King, Jr., had been assassinated in Memphis, Tennessee. Kennedy was advised to cancel his speech; tension was running high in the black community and there would be no guarantee of his safety. "There's no way I won't give that speech," he insisted. "I've got to make that speech. It's the most important thing I can do." When he arrived he stood on the back of a flatbed truck under an umbrella in the rain and leaned into the microphone. The crowd had not yet heard the news. "I have bad news for you, for all of our fellow citizens, and people who love peace all over the world, and that is that Martin Luther King was shot and killed tonight," Kennedy said. The crowd gasped in shock and horror. "Martin Luther King dedicated his life to love and to justice for his fellow human beings, and he died because of that effort," Kennedy continued. "In this difficult day, in this difficult time for the United States, it is perhaps well to ask what kind of nation we are and what direction we want to move in. For those of you who are black—considering the evidence there evidently is that there were white people who were responsible—you can be filled with bitterness, with hatred, and a desire for revenge. We can move in that direction as a country, in great polarization—black people amongst black, white people amongst white, filled with hatred toward one another. Or we can make an effort, as Martin Luther King did, to understand and to comprehend, and to replace that violence, that stain of bloodshed that has spread across our land, with an effort to understand with compassion and love." His voice broke as he said those words, and someone shouted "I love Bobby."

"For those of you who are black and are tempted to be filled with hatred and distrust at the injustice of such an act, against all white people, I can only say that I feel in my own heart the same kind of feeling. I had a member of my family killed, but he was killed by a white man. But we have to make an effort in the United States, we have to make an effort to understand, to go beyond these rather difficult times. . . . Let us dedicate ourselves to what the Greeks wrote so many years ago: to tame the savageness of man and to make gentle the life of this world. Let us dedicate ourselves to that, and say a prayer for our country and for our people."

There were no riots in Indianapolis that night. But there were riots in over 100 other cities. Forty-six people were killed, hundreds were injured, and over 20,000 people were arrested. Washington was under curfew and guarded by federal troops in gas masks. Kennedy stepped through burning timbers and over shattered glass in other parts of Indiana as he walked through the streets. Stores were looted and burned. Mrs. King was trying to get an airplane to bring her husband's body back to Atlanta. Afraid of notoriety, the airlines refused. Kennedy arranged for a private plane borrowed from a friend to bring Martin Luther King home, and he marched in his shirtsleeves at the funeral. "We marched at his funeral," Coretta Scott King said, "because Martin had spent so much of his life marching. . . . This was his last great march."[9]

Robert Kennedy for president (©Arlene Schulman)

Kennedy listened to people whose voices were rarely heard—poor blacks and whites, people without jobs, farmers, Indians on reservations suffering from alcoholism, Mexican-American migrant workers, college students protesting against the Vietnam War, Hispanics living in public housing projects, the children of the slums. "Perhaps we cannot prevent this world from being a world in which children are tortured," he said, quoting the writer Albert Camus. "But we can reduce the number of tortured children. And if you believers don't help us, who else in the world can help us do this?" In a speech in California, he said, "Our brave young men are dying in the swamps of Southeast Asia. Which one of them might have written a poem? Which one of them might have cured cancer? Which one of them might have played in a World Series or given us the gift of laughter from the stage or helped build a bridge or a university? Which of them would have taught a child to read? It is our responsibility to let these men live. . . . It is indecent if they die because of the empty vanity of their country."[10]

Students chanted, cheered, and stamped their feet. Priests and nuns who wore Kennedy bumper stickers across their cornets turned out and waved to him as he sat on the hood of the car. Hundreds of people walked or ran alongside of his convertible. People waited for hours to catch a glimpse of him or to touch him. "I found that they wanted not just to touch a celebrity; they wanted to convey their feelings to him, and he accepted it for that," said his security man, Bill Barry. He gave out tie clips shaped like PT boats just like his brother did. By the end of the day, his hands would be swollen and bleeding.

On May 7, the results of the Indiana primary were announced. Kennedy had won 42 percent of the vote to McCarthy's 27 percent. The white working-class vote had come out for Kennedy. When asked to explain this, Kennedy joked, "I think part of it is that Gene [Eugene McCarthy] comes across lace curtain Irish to these people. They can tell I'm pure shanty Irish."

The next contest took place in Nebraska. The Kennedy campaign, commented one reporter, became a "huge, joyous adventure." Another reporter spoke of Kennedy's "way of pulling individuals around him into his orbit, a strange disarming quality about him that somehow evoked sympathy." However, when a group of reporters discussed Kennedy's future, John J. Lindsay of *Newsweek* sounded an ominous note. "Of course, he has the stuff to go all the way," Lindsay observed. "But he's not going to go all the way. Somebody is going to shoot him. He's out there now waiting for him."[11]

Kennedy did not believe in security. "We can't have that kind of country—where the president of the United States is afraid to go among the people. I won't ride around in an armored car," he said. "If anyone wants to kill me, it won't be difficult."[12] He said that there were no guarantees against assassination. "You've just got to give yourself to the people and to trust them, and from then on . . . either [luck is] with you or it isn't. I am pretty sure there'll be an attempt on my life sooner or later. Not so much for political reasons," he added. "Plain nuttiness, that's all."[13]

The poet Robert Lowell recalled that "he felt he was doomed, and you knew that he felt that. . . . He knew that, and he had no middle course possible to him." Kennedy did hire former FBI special agent Bill Barry to accompany him, but Barry's main job was to get Kennedy through the crowds. Sometimes Barry tried to hire off-duty policemen to patrol the lobbies of hotels, but when Kennedy found out, he canceled them. "If things happen, they are going to happen," Kennedy said.[14] There were several alarms—men armed with guns, death threats—in Cleveland, in Salt Lake City, in California. Kennedy ignored them. He told a reporter that, yes, he had thought about it (assassination), but he wasn't going to change his campaign because of it. "I can't plan. Living every day is like Russian roulette," he said.[15]

That May, Kennedy threw a surprise party for Bill Barry in celebration of Barry's 41st birthday. Suddenly, a balloon popped, and it sounded like a gunshot. "It would have been a forgotten interlude," said Helen Dudar of the *New York Post*, "except for Kennedy's reaction; it was not a shellshock reflex and it almost proceeded in slow motion. The back of his hand came up toward his face, which was frowning, and he held his hand there, his head bent, for perhaps a count of ten. The party stood suspended in time for those seconds and then Kennedy came back from wherever he'd been and it resumed."[16]

Kennedy won the state of Nebraska with 51.5 percent of the vote, while McCarthy took 31 percent. But Kennedy lost the primary in Oregon, where McCarthy called him a spoiled child and ridiculed him. Employment was high in Oregon, and minorities were only 2 percent of the population. "Let's face it," Kennedy told a reporter, "I appeal best to people who have problems." Kennedy spoke of an America that had lost its way, but Oregonians did not feel that they had lost their way. Those opposed to the Vietnam War found McCarthy as forceful as Kennedy in denouncing U.S. policy.

Though he lost Oregon, Kennedy was able to court the state's small but influential population of Jews, knowing that he would need the Jewish vote in California and New York. At the time, half a million Palestinian Arabs had been displaced from their homes during the Six-Day War and were living in refugee camps in Lebanon, Jordan, and Syria. Kennedy never acknowledged the plight of the Arabs and often criticized them. At a meeting of Jewish labor leaders the year before, he had cleared his throat in a mock cough, made a face, and said, "I've just drunk a cup of bitter Arab coffee and have not had time to wash my mouth." In a speech at a synagogue in Oregon on May 26, Kennedy took a stronger position on Israel than any other U.S. presidential candidate had ever taken. "The U.S. must defend Israel against aggression from whatever source," Kennedy said. "Our obligations to Israel, unlike our obligations towards other countries, are clear and imperative. Israel is the very opposite of Vietnam. Israel's government is democratic, effective, free of corruption, its people united in its support." He added, "The United States should, without delay, sell Israel the fifty Phantom jets she has so long been promised."[17]

The next day, a photograph of Kennedy appeared in a Pasadena, California, paper, *The Independent*, to which a young Arab man named Sirhan Sirhan subscribed. The caption underneath the photograph read "BOBBY SAYS SHALOM—Sen. Robert F. Kennedy, wearing a traditional Jewish 'yarmulke,' addressed the Neveh Shalom congregation in Portland on his campaign tour of Oregon. He told the congregation the U.S. must support Israel against outside aggression." Sirhan wrote in his diary: "My determination to eliminate R.F.K. is becoming more of an unshakable obsession. . . . R.F.K. must die—R.F.K. must be killed, Robert F. Kennedy must be assassinated. . . . Robert F. Kennedy must be assassinated before June 5, '68."[18] (June 5 would be the first anniversary of the Six-Day War between Israel and neighboring Arab states.) Sirhan then bought four boxes of .22-caliber bullets for $3.99.

After the Oregon primary, Kennedy boarded a train for California, the next stop on the campaign trail. With 174 delegates at stake, California was crucial to Kennedy's drive for the nomination. He was greeted by Mexican Americans, mobbed by admirers in the black community of Watts, and spat on by opponents in San Francisco. "I am so well aware of being disliked," he said, "that it no longer surprises or disturbs me. I no longer care." California Democrats were divided, and Kennedy campaigned 20 hours a day. He debated McCarthy on June 1 in San Francisco for an hour on the local ABC affiliate. While McCarthy argued for eliminating ghettos, Kennedy called instead for their reconstruction. "Come by and explain to us what a terrific guy you are," McCarthy said, a little nastily. Kennedy said, "I am in favor of moving people out of the ghettos, but we have 14 million Negroes here in the ghetto at the present time. We have here in the State of California a million Mexican-Americans whose poverty is even greater than any of the black people's. I want to do things in the suburbs but what I am saying is in order to meet the really hard-core heart of the problem, we have to face the fact that a lot of these people are going to live here (in the ghettos) for another several decades. And they can't live under the conditions that they are living under at the present time." Critics called the debate a draw.

Television was playing an increasingly important role in politics, and McCarthy mounted a strong television campaign, particularly at the end of the primary. Kennedy appeared in five-minute campaign ads five nights a week, just before the 11 o'clock news, stating, "This is Robert Kennedy and I want to talk to the people of the nation just as I did to the people in the states with primaries." Kennedy also put together a half-hour program highlighting his speeches and his public life.

The Monday before the California primary, Kennedy traveled more than 1,200 miles throughout the state and met with members of almost every ethnic group. "Yes, you come out to see me. Are you just going to wave to Mr. Kennedy and then tomorrow when I'm gone forget about me, or are you going to vote?" he asked, teasing a supportive crowd in Watts.

June 4 was primary day, and blacks and Mexicans turned out in record numbers. In the Mexican-American communities, Kennedy supporters went door to door saying, "This is the day Cesar [Chavez] says to vote for Robert F. Kennedy." Fourteen out of 15 Mexican-American voters cast their ballots for Kennedy. In some black neighborhoods, nine out of every ten registered Democrats voted, a higher percentage than in many of the Jewish neighborhoods, which normally had the largest turnout.

Kennedy spent Election Day relaxing in Malibu. As he was swimming in the ocean with his 12-year-old son David, the boy was pulled under by a strong tide, and Kennedy had to rescue him. A little after seven in the evening, he arrived in his fifth-floor suite at the Ambassador Hotel in Los Angeles, where his election headquarters were set up. A few minutes later returns came in from the South Dakota primary, which had also been held that day. Even though South Dakota was Hubert Humphrey's birthplace, Kennedy won 50 percent of the vote to Humphrey's 30 percent and McCarthy's 20 percent. Kennedy was asked to explain his popularity. "I always say it's because I have charm and wit, and personality and ability," he replied. "But there may be something else to it."[19]

Two hours later Sirhan Sirhan parked his car nearby and entered the hotel. Dressed in jeans, a white shirt, and a blue sweater, he blended in with the rest of the Kennedy supporters who jammed the hotel. He had tucked a pistol into the top of his pants and pulled his sweater over it. He watched the election returns come in over the teletype along with the Kennedy campaign workers.

Kennedy watched the election returns with his family, friends, and aides in the Ambassador's Royal Suite. Because of a computer breakdown, the results were coming in with agonizing slowness. At 8:30, CBS announced Kennedy in the lead, while NBC had McCarthy leading. Half an hour later, a restless Kennedy paced the hallway and was questioned by a host of reporters. "I like politicians," Kennedy said. "I like politics. It's an honorable adventure."

At 11:30, the campaign workers and supporters downstairs in the Embassy Ballroom were getting restless too. They chanted, "We want Kennedy! We want Kennedy!" Ten minutes later, a shout of joy went up in the Royal Suite. The final returns were in, and Kennedy had triumphed over McCarthy by 46 percent to 42 percent. He lit up a small victory cigar.

Robert Kennedy gives his victory speech at the Ambassador Hotel, June 1968.
(Howard Decker/Photoreporters, Inc.)

"Finally I feel that I'm out from under the shadow of my brother," he told a friend. "Now at least I've made it on my own. All these years I never really believed it was me that did it, but Jack."[20]

A jubilant Robert Kennedy went down to the ballroom to thank his campaign workers and deliver his victory speech. He took the service elevator to the kitchen pantry and walked through a crowded corridor to the podium in the ballroom. He had no security, no one to clear the area as he passed through. Lieutenant Jack Eberhardt of the Los Angeles Police Department said that Kennedy "in no uncertain terms, told us he didn't care for our assistance. He felt that we were preventing him from getting a close rapport with his followers."[21] Neither Kennedy nor his staff sensed any danger. By the time Kennedy reached the podium, Sirhan was standing in the pantry area among a dozen kitchen workers, waiting for Kennedy to come through again.

Before a wildly cheering crowd, Kennedy thanked those who had helped him: "I want to express my gratitude to my dog Freckles. . . . I'm not doing this in any order of importance, but I also want to thank my wife Ethel. Her patience during this whole effort was fantastic. . . . All of the students who worked across the state. I want to thank Cesar Chavez, who was here a little earlier. And Bert Carona, who also worked with him, and all those Mexican-Americans who were great supporters of mine." The crowd cheered, blowing noisemakers and throwing hats into the air. "And Dolores Huerta, who is an old friend of mine, and has worked with the union. . . . I want to also thank my friends in the black community who made such an effort in this campaign. With such a high percentage voting today, I think it really made a major difference for me. I want to express my appreciation to them. . . . To my old friend, if I may, Rafer Johnson [the 1960 Olympic decathlon champion], who is here. And to [football player] Roosevelt Grier, who said that he'd take care of anybody who didn't vote for me." The crowd laughed along with Kennedy. "In a kind way, because that's the way we are. So I thank all of you who made all this possible. All of the effort that you made, and all of the people whose names I haven't mentioned, but who did all the work at the precinct level, who got out the vote. I was a campaign manager eight years ago. I know what a difference that kind of effort, and that kind of commitment made. I thank all of you."

As Kennedy was delivering his victory speech, Sirhan, his gun now concealed in a roll of heavy paper, climbed up on a tray stacker in the pantry area and crouched down. A security guard would have spotted him, but because there was no security, Sirhan went unnoticed.

"What I think is quite clear," Kennedy said, "is that we can work together in the last analysis, and that what has been going on within the United States over a period of the last three years—the division, the violence, the disenchantment with our society: the divisions, whether it's between blacks and whites, between the poor and the more affluent, or between age groups or on the war in Vietnam—is that we can start to work together. We are a great country, an unselfish country, and a compassionate country. I intend to make that my basis for running."[22]

Kennedy concluded by flashing that Kennedy smile and making a V-for-victory sign with his fingers. "Mayor [Sam] Yorty [of Los Angeles] has just sent me a message that we've been here too long already," he said. "So my thanks to all of you, and on to Chicago, and let's win there!"

The crowd again took up the chant, "We want Kennedy! We want Kennedy!"

Kennedy left the podium and reentered the crowded serving pantry, where he began shaking hands with the busboys and kitchen helpers. It was fifteen minutes after midnight. When Kennedy approached, Sirhan uncovered his pistol, jumped down from the tray stacker, and fired.

Three bullets struck Robert Kennedy. As he lay mortally wounded near a sign that read "The Once and Future King," Sirhan continued to fire, wounding five others. It took eight people to subdue Sirhan and wrench the gun out of his hand. Sirhan cried out, "I can explain . . . let me explain . . . I did it for my country . . . I love my country."

Hysteria swept the ballroom. Some people collapsed, others prayed. A black man pounded the wall, shouting, "Why, God, why? Why again? Why another Kennedy?"

Juan Romero, a busboy who had been shaking Kennedy's hand when Sirhan fired, attempted to raise the senator's head. Ethel Kennedy rushed to her husband's side. "No, God! It can't be!"

Robert Kennedy, as he lay mortally wounded   (Bill Eppridge, *Life* magazine,
© Time Inc.)

a voice cried out. Romero took a set of rosary beads, placed it
in Kennedy's hands and prayed quietly. "Is everybody okay?"
Kennedy whispered.

The next morning, 11-year-old Robert Kennedy, Jr., went
downstairs at the family home in Hickory Hill to pick up the
paper. The headline said that his father had been shot in Los
Angeles. He took the paper inside and burned it in the fireplace.

Later that night, June 6, 1968, 26 hours after the shooting, Robert F. Kennedy died at Good Samaritan Hospital in Los Angeles. He was 42.

Notes

1. Robert F. Kennedy, *The Enemy Within* (New York: Harper, 1963), p. 185.
2. Jules Witcover, *Eighty-five Days: The Last Campaign of Robert Kennedy* (New York: Morrow, 1969), p. 79.
3. William vanden Heuvel and Milton Gwirtzman, *On His Own: RFK 1964–68* (Garden City, N.Y.: Doubleday, 1970), p. 209.
4. Jack Newfield, *Robert Kennedy: A Memoir* (New York: New American Library, 1969), p. 56.
5. NBC, *Robert F. Kennedy: The Man and the Memories*, May 28, 1993.
6. Interview with the author, December 1996.
7. Edwin O. Guthman and C. Richard Allen, *RFK: Collected Speeches* (New York: Viking, 1993), p. 206.
8. Speech, Kansas State University, March 18, 1968.
9. Witcover, *Eighty-five Days*, p. 114.
10. Arthur Schlesinger, Jr., *Robert Kennedy and His Times* (Boston: Houghton Mifflin, 1978), p. 864.
11. Schlesinger, *Robert Kennedy and His Times*, p. 900.
12. Bill Eppridge and Hays Gorey, *Robert Kennedy: The Last Campaign* (New York: Harcourt Brace, 1993), p. 125.
13. Schlesinger, *Robert Kennedy and His Times*, p. 901.
14. Schlesinger, *Robert Kennedy and His Times*, p. 901.
15. Victor Lasky, *Robert F. Kennedy: The Myth and the Man* (New York: Trident Press, 1968), p. 339.
16. Schlesinger, *Robert Kennedy and His Times*, p. 902.
17. John H. Davis, *The Kennedys: Dynasty and Disaster* (New York: McGraw-Hill, 1984), pp. 654–55.
18. Davis, *The Kennedys*, p. 658.
19. Lasky, *Robert F. Kennedy: The Myth and the Man*, p. 339.
20. Davis, *The Kennedys*, p. 350.
21. Schlesinger, *Robert Kennedy and His Times*, p. 901.
22. Schlesinger, *Robert Kennedy and His Times*, p. 914.

7

THE LEGACY CONTINUES

The news traveled quickly across the country and around the world. In many inner-city communities, people wept openly. Churches filled up in Ireland, and flags flew at half-mast. In Vietnam, Second Lieutenant Lawrence Patch of Topeka, Kansas, said, "It was a horrible tragedy. But it has more meaning for us serving over here than for those back in the United States."

"I have an empty feeling," said Navy Lieutenant Steven C. Taylor of St. Louis, Missouri. "I'm supposed to go home in ten days. Now I just don't look forward to seeing the States as much as I have the past 16 months."[1]

On the evening of the primary in California, Rose Kennedy had gone to bed early. She heard the news when she woke up the next morning. "I really don't remember what I was thinking," she wrote in her autobiography, "except that I was praying 'Lord Have Mercy,' and thinking, 'Oh, Bobby, Bobby, Bobby.'"[2] "It seemed impossible that the same kind of disaster could befall our family twice in five years," she wrote. "If I had read anything of the sort in fiction I would have put it aside as incredible."[3]

Rose was concerned about Robert's wife, Ethel. "She and Bobby loved each other deeply—they loved being together, sharing everything; they had a perfect life. Much as I would grieve for Bobby and miss him, I knew she would miss him even more: not only for all they meant to each other but as the father of her ten children, with the eleventh to come posthumously a few months later. I knew how difficult it was going to be for her to raise that big family without the guiding role and influence that Bobby would have provided."[4]

Robert's last child, named Rory Kathleen Elizabeth, was born in 1969. Ted Kennedy was now a father to 16 children—his own three, the two children of his brother John, and Robert's 11.

As Robert Kennedy's body lay in state in St. Patrick's Cathedral in New York City, the line of mourners stretched for more than a mile. More than 150,000 people filed past the coffin, many crossing themselves and weeping. Thousands of onlookers lined Fifth Avenue. Ted Kennedy delivered the eulogy on June 8, 1968: "My brother need not be idealized, or enlarged in death beyond what he was in life, to be remembered simply as a good and decent man, who saw wrong and tried to right it, saw suffering and tried to heal it, saw war and tried to stop it. Those of us who loved him and who take him to his rest today pray that what he was to us and what he wished for others will someday come to pass for all the world. As he said many times, in many parts of this nation, to those he touched and who sought to touch him:

> 'Some men see things as they are and say why,
> I dream things that never were and say why not.'"[5]

Delivering a eulogy on the floor of the Senate on July 30, 1968, Senator Jacob Javits said, "He had deep concern for the people whom our society . . . had disenfranchised in terms of opportunity and in terms of the legacy to which we feel all Americans are entitled. He was not the only man in public life to have this feeling in his heart; but, in my judgment, it burned in him more brightly than in any other man I have ever known."[6]

A 21-car train carried Kennedy's coffin from New York City to his final resting place at Arlington National Cemetery in Virginia. More than a million people lined the path of the funeral train. Men and women, black and white, held up their children, waved American flags, and saluted. Some sang "The Battle Hymn of the Republic," and there were many signs:

PRAY FOR US, BOBBY
GOD BLESS THE KENNEDYS
GOOD-BYE, BOBBY
BOBBY, WE'LL MISS YOU
WE HAVE LOST OUR LAST HOPE

Robert F. Kennedy, Jr., later recalled, "One of the most poignant memories that I have of the impact of my father's political career was after he died, I was inside in the train and almost continuously the whole way, the train tracks were just packed with people. There were all kinds of people, a lot of them were crying, a lot of them were waving signs that said, 'GOOD-BYE, BOBBY.'"[7]

Robert Kennedy was buried under a simple white cross on a hillside overlooking the eternal flame that marks his brother's grave.

Sirhan Sirhan was found guilty of premeditated murder in the first degree with recommendation of the death penalty. Ted Kennedy pleaded for leniency, and Sirhan was sentenced to life in prison with the possibility of parole. He has never been granted parole.

Kennedy once visited the Pine Ridge Indian Reservation in Lakota, South Dakota, and the editor of the local newspaper, *The Lakota Times*, publishes a story about his visit every other year in commemoration of that visit. "It was almost as if a saint had come and was reaching his hand to the people," the editor recalled. "He went to the grubbiest children and hugged and kissed them."[8]

"He became the champion of the poor, the blacks, the Indians," wrote the newspaper columnist Mary McGrory after his death. "Although possessed of advantages, he felt himself as one of the disadvantaged. He had been dispossessed of his treasure, his brother."[9]

Newsweek columnist Kenneth Crawford wrote that "[Kennedy's] vitality, courage and spirited policy line had made him an irreplaceable factor, whether he won or lost the Democratic nomination."

Roosevelt Grier, the football player who was alongside Kennedy when he was killed, also expressed his sense of loss. "Everyone felt that they had a part in rebuilding. It wasn't Bobby's America, or a white America or a black America, it was our America," he said. "When you're a soldier fighting for causes, you don't know what's going to happen. He had to go out and risk everything he had. We were on our way. I always think," he added, his voice trailing off, "if we had gone the other way [instead of taking a shortcut through the kitchen] . . ."[10]

Dolores Huerta of the United Farm Workers Association recalled, "The night he got killed I was the person standing next to him. He just won the primary. It was a very joyous moment which was very, very short-lived. We hoped that the shot wasn't fatal, that he would survive. It's hard to get over. We were very, very saddened. . . . [Robert Kennedy] taught me the importance of what one person can do in the political realm and the importance of the individual and his influence. He had an incredible amount of energy and a very distinctive look on life. He was thirty years ahead of his time. All of the strikers said, 'This is a man who has some guts.' The fact that he's not here, I just want to cry."[11]

"Death has a way of making people more heroic," said Jeff Greenfield, a former legislative aide to Kennedy and an ABC News political analyst. He recalled interviewing a South African leader in the mid-80s who drove around the streets of Soweto with a soundtrack blaring the speeches of Robert Kennedy and Martin Luther King. "'Each time a man stands up for an ideal, or acts to improve the lot of others, or strikes out against injustice, he sends forth a tiny ripple of hope, and crossing each other from a million different centers of energy and daring, those ripples build a current that can sweep down the mightiest walls of oppression and resistance.' . . . He was seen as a hero. He had both an intellectual and emotional commitment. A lot of people didn't ordinarily trust politicians. He was able to get people convinced that politics might make a difference. He kept the coalition together. He had the ability to be a passionate advocate and not be seen as a threat to whites. People didn't always agree with him but he meant what he said. I have no idea if he would have won in 1968. A lot of states were for Humphrey. What I do believe is that at the age of 42 he had an enormous impact on politics. There's no one pushing, no one challenging. You see the loss most clearly. . . . I think of him whenever I go out and cover a campaign."[12]

John Lewis, a Georgia congressman and a civil rights activist, has said that he "probably wouldn't be where I am if it weren't for Robert Kennedy. More than any other politician of my time . . . he inspired a whole breed of young people to get into politics. I saw in his campaign a sense of daring, a sense of courage that said if you really believe in something, you've got to fight for it. He had the ability to go straight to the heart of an issue, like civil rights or Vietnam. And his tie with blacks, there was nothing false about it. Black voters who with others would be unresponsive sensed something about Bobby Kennedy that was different from any other politician. He was able to communicate not only with his lips but with his heart and guts. Those of us who came through the civil rights movement dealt with him on a different level. We knew him as a fighter, standing up for the little man in the South and in South Africa."[13]

In June 1993, 25 years after Robert Kennedy's assassination, President Bill Clinton spoke at a memorial mass at Arlington National Cemetery: "He spoke out against neglect, but he challenged the neglected to seize their own destiny. He wanted so badly for Government to act, but he did not trust bureaucracy. And he believed that Government had to do things with people, not for them. He knew we had to do things together or not at all. . . . When he was alive, some said that he was ruthless; some said he wasn't a real liberal, and others claimed he was a real radical. If he were here today, I think he would laugh and say they were both right. But now as we see him more clearly, we understand he was a man who was very gentle to those who were most vulnerable, very tough in the standards he kept for himself, very old-fashioned in the virtues in which he believed, and a relentless searcher for change, for growth, for the potential of heart and mind that he sought in himself and he demanded of others."[14]

Arthur Schlesinger, Jr., a biographer of Robert Kennedy and of his brother John, feels that Kennedy's assassination changed the course of U.S. politics: "He would have been elected President. We would have gotten out of Vietnam in 1969, not 1972. He was very much interested in the schools. If he had been elected there would not have been a Watergate [the scandal that caused President Nixon to resign in 1974]. He would have done more for the country than any other person. His general attitude was with the weak, disenfranchised and the powerless. We could give everyone a better chance at life. He embodied the underclass. I think people miss it and value that memory. He was a passionate man."[15]

Charles Evers, the brother of slain civil rights leader Medgar Evers, said, "Robert Kennedy was ruthless, all right. He was ruthless against wrong, against racketeers and hatemongers.

He was ruthlessly dedicated to the welfare of all people. If he had become President, he would have been President of all the people, but especially of the poor and disadvantaged. We would have seen, during his four or eight years, a change in America that we can hardly conceive of now, a change in the whole atmosphere."[16]

"In the end I thought what mattered most was his effort to give a divided society a common vision," wrote Anthony Lewis in the *New York Times*. "Somehow he convinced those outside the system, the dispossessed and disaffected, that they could find a place inside. He told those who were inside that they had a responsibility for the whole. . . . Robert Kennedy cared, and it made a difference. Somehow, almost wordlessly, he was able to communicate to people that he understood their troubles and sympathized: not as a politician but as a human being."[17]

A senator since 1962, Ted Kennedy has kept Robert's ideals alive, denouncing the Vietnam War and championing bills on such issues as civil rights, national health insurance, gun control legislation, child care, nutritional labeling, job training, expansion of Head Start, and fair housing. His future as a presidential candidate was damaged in 1969 when he drove his car off a small bridge in Chappaquiddick, Massachusetts. The accident resulted in the death of Kennedy's passenger, Mary Jo Kopechne, and Kennedy was severely criticized for leaving the scene of the accident and not calling the police until the following day. After an unsuccessful bid for the Democratic nomination in 1980, he abandoned any thought of achieving the White House.

Joseph P. Kennedy died in 1969 at the age of 81 with a fortune estimated at $100 million. When he died, an editorial in the *Boston Herald* said of him: "In his own right and on his own terms, Joseph P. Kennedy rose from modest beginnings to the pinnacles of financial power and political eminence by adhering to old-fashioned American virtues that have been somewhat discounted in today's society: devotion to family, loyalty to friends, strength of character, and the will to win." His grandson and namesake remarked that "the only reason any of us can afford to go into politics, human rights and environmental law is our grandfather went out and made a lot of money for all of us."[18]

In 1984, David Kennedy, Robert Kennedy's fourth son, died at the age of 28 of a drug overdose. He is buried next to Joseph P. Kennedy in the family plot in Brookline. Jacqueline Kennedy Onassis died in May 1994. Rose Kennedy died at the age of 104 in January 1995.

The large mahogany desk that Robert Kennedy used when he was attorney general was given to his oldest son, Joe, a congressman from Massachusetts, who was 16 when his father was assassinated. "It's great to have my dad's desk," he said. "It's going to bring back a lot of great memories. A lot of great things happened while my dad sat at that desk."[19] He said on another occasion, "As the years pile up since his terrible premature death, there is a tendency to polish the sharp edges of the man. He did not lead by giving smooth and soothing assurances. He made us feel uncomfortable and he was prickly and impatient and told us we would have to change and sacrifice."[20]

Robert and Ethel Kennedy's oldest child, Kathleen Kennedy Townsend, was elected lieutenant governor of Maryland in 1995. "He understood suffering, and a lot of people were suffering," she said of her father. "In the way John Kennedy in running for President tried to raise the level of people's ideas, my father talked about suffering in a way that resonated deeply in people's hearts, until they felt something larger than themselves. And it was not just talking about getting things done. Like Bedford-Stuyvesant, he got them done."[21]

Robert F. Kennedy, Jr., became a professor of environmental law and an environmental activist in New York. "A lot of this comes from my father," he said of his work. "My father, probably because he had money, didn't value money much, and he taught us to be people of values more than people of success. We learned about duty and we all bought into it."[22]

The Robert F. Kennedy Memorial was established in 1968 by family and friends and sponsors annual book and journalism awards. It has funded both the RFK National Juvenile Justice Project and the Washington Juvenile Justice Project. Kerry Kennedy Cuomo founded the Kennedy Memorial's Center for Human Rights and initiated its Human Rights Awards, which have recognized and supported human rights advocates around the world. "My father talked about children suffering," said Kerry Kennedy Cuomo. "He did inspire us in the way that we were brought up. Public service was quite central to our family."[23]

Robert Kennedy left behind a powerful legacy in Bedford-Stuyvesant. There are still plenty of problems in the neighborhood, but the Bedford-Stuyvesant Restoration Project has spurred more than $450 million in private investments. Thousands of jobs have been created since Kennedy's death, and hundreds of brownstones and tenements have been restored. Two community centers have been opened, offering legal counseling and free advice. The Restoration Project also played a leading role in the creation of Medgar Evers College, which celebrated its 25th anniversary in 1995. (The establishment of a college with close ties to the community was Kennedy's idea.) Although IBM has moved out of the area, the factory was bought by its workers. The complex of buildings that is home to Bedford-Stuyvesant Restoration now houses the Billie Holiday Theatre, a skating rink, an art gallery, a post office, and shops.

Robert F. Kennedy, Jr., and his son, Robert F. Kennedy III, 12, distribute Christmas gifts in Bedford-Stuyvesant. Also in the photograph are Kennedy's wife, Mary Richardson; son Conor, two; and daughter Kyra, one. The little blonde girl is nine-year-old daughter Kathleen's friend Annie Starke. (© Arlene Schulman)

Under the Restoration Project's sponsorship, children and teenagers participate in acting, dancing, and art classes. The Youth Development Leadership Institute provides a 13-week course of leadership training and an entrepreneurship program that teaches the operations of a business, basic banking skills, and customer service. Other important facilities include the Computer Tutorial and Homework Assistance Center, the Restoration Mass Choir, and the Restoration Dance Theatre, which performed at the 1996 Olympics in Atlanta.

Lasia Young, a graduate of the Youth Development Leadership Institute, said, "I've learned how to handle situations with different people. I learned how to fix my resume. It has built my confidence and made me more aware of things out there for me. It has broadened my horizons." John Williams, a high school student with plans to be a computer scientist, added, "I learned how you look, how you dress, how you speak, it gives you the first impression. I learned about the negatives and positives of peer pressure, the effect of good resume writing. I learned how to plan for the future. Before I came here, I never thought about what I wanted to do, where I was going. It gives you a different way of looking at life. I'm looking through another pair of eyes."[24]

Ethel Kennedy attends many of the meetings of the Restoration Corporation, and both she and Robert Kennedy, Jr., are on the board of directors. Robert, Jr., and his family attend the annual Christmas party, handing out shopping bags full of gifts to neighborhood children. On one occasion, when his daughter passed a bust of Robert Kennedy with a friend, she proudly pointed out, "That's my granddad."

Clara and Horace Cannadate received a loan from Restoration as part of its revolving loan program. "His coming to Bed-Stuy was one of the best things he could ever do," said Horace Cannadate. "It still has an impact. Bed-Stuy is not the same." Cannadate and his wife opened a successful take-out restaurant, Carolina Creek, in 1990 but soon found themselves in need of cash to replace failing equipment. "We were paying so much money in repairs," Clara Cannadate recalled. "The freezer kept going down. We didn't have the money to do it. We went everywhere. We went to all the banks but they said that we had to be in business for five years. We were in business for three. Someone recommended that we go over to Restoration and we did. We did a business plan—not only did they approve it but they gave us what we asked for. They were just outstanding. We were so used to hearing 'We can't do anything for you.' We said we needed $50,000. We got the $50,000. We bought a new refrigerator/freezer, a cash register, a rotisserie and warmer, scales, and other things that we needed. It's been a blessing."[25]

In turn, the Cannadates help others. They offer advice and encouragement to other entrepreneurs, and high school students work with them after school. They hired a young man who had been released from prison on a work-release program. "We opened our home to him," said Clara Cannadate. "He's been with us from day one. Another was living on the street for six years. He's been straight since he's been with us. His mother didn't even recognize him. I took him to get a peddler's license and now he's getting ready to buy his own home."

Across the river in East Harlem, Thelma Hall lamented the absence of Kennedy's leadership when so much remained to be done. "He was campaigning here and he came up Third Avenue in a flatbed truck," she recalled. "I'll never forget that. No candidate ever came this way. You don't go to this neighborhood. You go downtown and people pay thousands of dollars for a dinner. He reached down and touched people. People were very excited. I was, too. He made me feel of value. You were counted. You were important. He was interested in people—period. He fought for the country as a whole—not just me. I, too, was a people. I really wanted him to be elected. Oh, God! I was totally devastated [when he died]. I cried. I was very upset. There was an era gone. Look, if you're going to be in a war, you can't hide in a tent. You have to get out there. He was very idealistic and willing to put it into action. He was interested in changing things, in righting wrongs. You got the distinct feeling that this was going to be a new day and you wanted to be a part of it. I think the civil rights movement would have taken a different turn. Now, who's looking after us now?"[26]

Notes

1. Associated Press, June 6, 1968.
2. Rose Fitzgerald Kennedy, *Times to Remember* (Garden City, N.Y.: Doubleday, 1974), p. 476.
3. Kennedy, *Times to Remember*, p. 475.

4. Kennedy, *Times to Remember*, p. 477.
5. *New York Times*, June 9, 1968.
6. *New York Times*, July 31, 1968.
7. NBC, *Robert F. Kennedy: The Man and the Memories*, May 28, 1993.
8. *Time*, May, 9, 1988.
9. Jules Witcover, *Eighty-five Days: The Last Campaign of Robert Kennedy* (New York: Morrow, 1969), p. 333.
10. Interview with the author, November 1996.
11. Interview with the author, November 1996.
12. Interview with the author, October 1996.
13. Witcover, *Eighty-five Days*, p. 348.
14. *Weekly Compilation of Presidential Documents*, June 14, 1993, p. 1038.
15. Interview with the author, October 1996.
16. Pierre Salinger, ed. *An Honorable Profession: A Tribute to Robert F. Kennedy* (Garden City, N.Y.: Doubleday, 1968), p. 125.
17. *New York Times*, May 31, 1993.
18. *Chicago Sun Times*, March 13, 1994.
19. *Boston Globe*, May 18, 1994.
20. *Los Angeles Times*, May 15, 1993.
21. Witcover, *Eighty-five Days*, p. 346.
22. *Boston Globe*, May 21, 1993.
23. Interview with the author, November 1996.
24. Interviews with the author, December 1996.
25. Interview with the author, November 1996.
26. Interview with the author, October 1996.

BIBLIOGRAPHY

Adler, Bill. *Kids' Letters to President Kennedy*. New York: William Morrow, 1963.

Bernstein, Irving. *Promises Kept: John F. Kennedy's New Frontier*. New York: Oxford University Press, 1991.

Brinkley, David. *A Memoir*. New York: Alfred A. Knopf, 1995.

David, Lester, and Irene David. *Bobby Kennedy: The Making of a Folk Hero*. New York: Dodd, Mead & Co., 1986.

Davis, John H. *The Kennedys: Dynasty and Disaster*. New York: McGraw-Hill, 1984.

Eppridge, Bill, and Hays Gorey. *Robert Kennedy: The Last Campaign*. New York: Harcourt Brace & Company, 1993.

Fairlie, Henry. *The Kennedy Promise*. Garden City, N.Y.: Doubleday & Company, 1973.

Gitlin, Todd. *The Sixties: Years of Hope, Days of Rage*. New York: Bantam, 1993.

Goldfarb, Ronald. *Perfect Villains, Imperfect Heroes*. New York: Random House, 1995.

Goodwin, Doris Kearns. *The Fitzgeralds and the Kennedys: An American Saga*. New York: Simon & Schuster, 1987.

Guthman, Edwin O. *We Band of Brothers*. New York: Harper & Row, 1971.

Guthman, Edwin O., and C. Richard Allen. *RFK: Collected Speeches*. New York: Viking, 1993.

Guthman, Edwin O., and Jeffrey Shulman, editors. *Robert Kennedy in His Own Words*. New York: Bantam Press, 1988.

Halberstam, David. *The Unfinished Odyssey of Robert Kennedy*. New York: Bantam, 1969.

Hoffa, James R. *Hoffa: The Real Story*. New York: Stein and Day, 1976.

Johnson, Lyndon Baines. *The Vantage Point*. New York: Holt, Rinehart & Winston, 1971.

Kennedy, Robert F. *The Enemy Within*. New York: Greenwood Press, 1960.

———. *The Pursuit of Justice*. New York: Harper & Row, 1964.

———. *To Seek a Newer World*. New York: Doubleday & Company, 1967.

———. *Thirteen Days*. New York: W.W. Norton & Company, 1969.

Kennedy, Rose Fitzgerald. *Times to Remember*. Garden City, N.Y.: Doubleday & Co., 1974.

Kessler, Ronald. *The Sins of the Father: Joseph P. Kennedy and the Dynasty He Founded*. New York: Warner Books, 1996.

Koskoff, David E. *Joseph P. Kennedy: A Life and Times*. Englewood Cliffs, N.J.: Prentice-Hall, Inc., 1974.

Lasky, Victor. *Robert F. Kennedy: The Myth and the Man*. New York: Trident Press, 1968.

Manchester, William. *The Death of a President*. New York: Harper & Row, 1967.

———. *Portrait of a President*. Boston: Little, Brown and Company, 1962.

———. *Remembering Kennedy: One Brief Shining Moment*. Boston: Little, Brown and Company, 1983.

Melanson, Philip H., Ph.D. *The Robert F. Kennedy Assassination*. New York: Shapolsky Publishers, 1991.

Moldea, Dan E. *The Killing of Robert F. Kennedy*. New York: W.W. Norton & Company, 1995.

Morrow, Robert D. *The Senator Must Die*. Santa Monica, Calif.: Roundtable Publishing, Inc., 1988.

Navasky, Victor S. *Kennedy Justice*. New York: Atheneum Publishers, 1971.

Newfield, Jack. *Robert Kennedy: A Memoir*. New York: New American Library, 1969.

Oppenheimer, Jerry. *The Other Mrs. Kennedy*. New York: St. Martin's Press, 1994.

Oshinsky, David M. *A Conspiracy So Immense: The World of Joe McCarthy*. New York: The Free Press/Macmillan, 1983.

Reeves, Richard. *President Kennedy: A Profile of Power*. New York: Touchstone, 1994.

Reston, James. *Deadline*. New York: Random House, 1991.

Rogers, Warren. *When I Think of Bobby: A Personal Memoir of the Kennedy Years*. New York: HarperCollins, 1993.

Schapp, Dick. *R.F.K.* New York: New American Library, 1967.

Schlesinger, Arthur, Jr. *Robert Kennedy and His Times*. Boston: Houghton Mifflin Company, 1978.

————. *A Thousand Days: John F. Kennedy in the White House.* Boston: Houghton Mifflin Company, 1965.

Sorenson, Theodore C. *The Kennedy Legacy.* New York: Macmillan, 1969.

Stein, Jean. *American Journey: The Times of Robert Kennedy.* New York: New American Library, 1970.

Summers, Anthony. *The Secret Life of J. Edgar Hoover.* New York: G.P. Putnam & Sons, 1993.

vanden Heuvel, William, and Milton Gwirtzman. *On His Own: RFK 1964–68.* Garden City, N.Y.: Doubleday & Co., 1970.

White, Theodore H. *The Making of the President 1960.* New York: Atheneum Publishers, 1961.

Witcover, Jules. *Eighty-five Days: The Last Campaign of Robert Kennedy.* New York: William Morrow, 1968.

Wofford, Harris. *Of Kennedys and Kings: Making Sense of the Sixties.* New York: Farrar, Straus & Giroux, 1980.

INDEX

Italic numbers indicate illustrations.